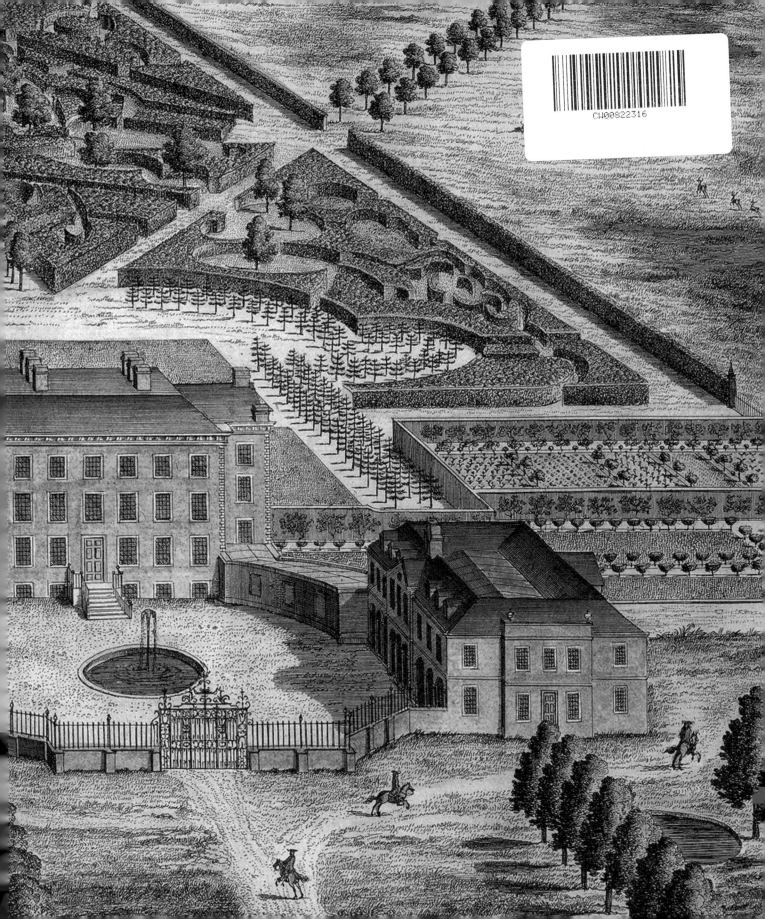

CW00822316

CHEVENING

A Seat of Diplomacy

CHEVENING

A Seat of Diplomacy

Julius Bryant

PAUL HOLBERTON PUBLISHING

Copyright © 2017
Text copyright © the author
All illustrations © The Trustees of Chevening 2017 except where otherwise stated

All rights reserved. No part of this publication may be transmitted in any form or by any means,
electronic or mechanical, including photocopy, recording or any storage or retrieval system,
without the prior permission in writing from the copyright holder and publisher.

ISBN 978 1 911300 11 3

British Library Cataloguing in Publication Data

A catalogue record for this book is available from the British Library

Produced by Paul Holberton Publishing
89 Borough High Street, London SE1 1NL
WWW.PAULHOLBERTON.COM

Photography by Richard Valencia and Hattie Young (2017)
and Matthew Hollow and Christopher Simon Sykes (2005)

'A Walk in the Park' and Stanhope Genealogy by MLDesign

Book design by Laura Parker

Printing by E-Graphic Srl, Verona

FRONT COVER: *Chevening, 2009, oil on canvas by Marcus May (detail)*
BACK COVER: *Chevening, 2017, photograph by Hattie Young*
ENDPAPERS: *Aerial view of Chevening, 1719, by Thomas Badeslade, engraved by Johannes Kip*
FRONTISPIECE: *Portraits of King George I, of James, 1st Earl Stanhope and of Thomas Pitt look down on the Great Hall*
PAGE 144: *A Reminiscence of a Delightful Day at Chevening, 14 September 1866, by E.M. Ward*

CONTENTS

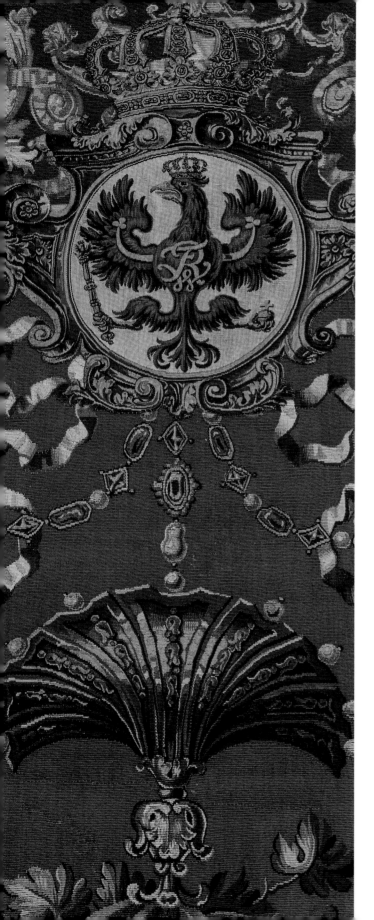

PREFACE

The occasion for this publication is Chevening's double anniversary in 2017 – three centuries since the 1st Earl Stanhope acquired the house and its surrounding estate in 1717; fifty years since the death in 1967 of the seventh and last Earl Stanhope, which brought into effect the Chevening Estate Act (1959).

Chevening has been the country home of the Foreign Secretary for several decades. It differs from the Prime Minister's country residence at Chequers and from the Chancellor of the Exchequer's at Dorneywood in several particulars. Chief among them is the extent of the Chevening Estate, which covers 3,000 acres, and the stewardship of the land by the Board of Trustees, exercising the powers of ownership vested in it by Parliament, which have ensured Chevening's independence from Government and from public funding. Of the three houses and estates Chevening is the finest, architecturally, historically and aesthetically, distinguished also by its Stanhope family connections and by the superb ancestral collections that make it such a rare (and fragile) entity.

Sir Winston Churchill described Chevening in 1943 as "this princely gift". Thanks to the donor, the last Earl Stanhope, it has found a continuing

The arms of Prussia on the tapestry representing Winter,
from the diplomatic gift presented by Friedrich Wilhelm
of Prussia to James, 1st Earl Stanhope in Berlin, 1720

role as a vital centre of the political life of this country. In moving the passage of the Chevening Estate Bill in the House of Commons on 19 June 1959, the Home Secretary, R.A. Butler, made the following observations:

"The Stanhope family have occupied the house for seven generations, since the first earl was first Minister of George I. The present Lord Stanhope, who had been in his time Lord President, Minister of Education and First Lord of the Admiralty, has wished that his family house and estate shall be able to continue in the service of the nation. He has felt for some time that this fine creation represented something that ought not to be allowed to perish, something which had indeed an enhanced value among the pressures, the stresses and the haste of modern times, and that Chevening should continue to make a contribution to the values of civilisation.

"Judging, perhaps rightly, that Ministers were among the greatest sufferers from these stresses and strains, in 1943 he informed the Prime Minister, then Mr. Winston Churchill, that he proposed to leave the estate and the house to the nation. The Prime Minister at once accepted what he described as "this princely gift". I wish now to thank Lord Stanhope on behalf of the nation, and I hope on behalf of the House, for his splendid generosity.

"The house lies in a tract of land of great natural beauty, partly wooded and covering several thousand acres. It is spacious but not overwhelming and it is a building of unusual charm, the designs of which are attributed to Inigo Jones. It conveys an atmosphere of restfulness and peace. Successive generations have extended and improved the house and added to it and to its treasures, which include the most intimate pictures of Lord Chatham, who occupied the house in 1769, and of his sons the second Earl and the younger Pitt. There is a letter of Lord Rosebery's written to the present owner's mother in 1911, in this very month of June, in which he has crossed out the address 'Chevening' and written 'Paradise'. In the library are originals of Stanhope's life of Pitt and Mahon's history of England. One pictures Mr Baldwin, who often visited Chevening, browsing among the volumes of literature and choosing apt quotations for the next week's debate."

As the home and frequently the workplace of successive Foreign Secretaries since 1980 the house has also lent its name to the United Kingdom's international awards scheme for developing future leaders through Chevening Scholarships and Chevening Fellowships.

Today, after fifty years of careful stewardship, Chevening is ready to fulfil the vital role that Stanhope, Churchill and Butler envisaged, as both a setting conducive to successful international diplomacy and a perfect example of one this country's classic contributions to global culture, the British country house.

CHAPTER ONE

A Tour of the House

INTRODUCTION

To the forecourt (fig. 1) Chevening presents a handsome face, all symmetry, order and harmony between its enclosing pavilion wings. Turning, we admire rolling pasture stretching to the North Downs of Kent, where the high, well-wooded horizon is broken by a distant 'keyhole' feature, cut in the beech-woods directly opposite the house (figs. 3 and 4). This serene prospect is veiled by a sweep of fine iron railings embellished at the gateposts with the Stanhope cypher and coronets (fig. 2). The classic, calm character of this English country house, an architectural ensemble of peace, privacy and security, must have comforted General James Stanhope (1673–1721; figs. 36, 107), following his early retirement from front-line fighting abroad. His army career had ended in defeat, as a prisoner of war, locked up in Spain for nearly two years.

Back in England in 1712, aged forty, Stanhope re-entered politics, found an heiress, Lucy Pitt, aged twenty-two, and married her six months after his return (fig. 11). By 1717 he had risen to be chief minister to King George I and had a house in Whitehall, leased from the government. On 15 June 1717 he purchased Chevening, an early seventeenth-century house with 3,466 acres, from the daughters of the Earl of Sussex, who had died

FIG. 2
The Stanhope cypher and coronet on the forecourt screen by Zachariah Gisbourn

FIG. 1 (FACING)
Chevening, the entrance and forecourt

FIG. 3
The view from the forecourt towards 'the keyhole'

FIG. 4 (FACING)
Chevening, as seen from 'the keyhole'

deep in debt. Most of the payment came from the dowry of Stanhope's young wife. A fortnight later, on 3 July 1717, he was elevated to the peerage, as Viscount Stanhope of Mahon and the following year he was created Earl Stanhope. He invested in enlarging the house and fathered seven children in eight years, but he did not have long to enjoy his personal paradise before his sudden death in 1721. His widow continued their improvements to Chevening.

The same year that Stanhope purchased Chevening, the architect Colen Campbell illustrated its elevations and floor plans in the second volume of his book *Vitruvius Britannicus* (1717; fig. 6). The general accuracy of these engravings is confirmed by a view of the house, with plans, in an estate map dated 1679 (fig. 5). The house had been rebuilt in the 1620s for the 13th Lord Dacre. In his text Campbell noted that Chevening "is said to be designed by Inigo Jones", the 'British Vitruvius' of his book's title. This traditional attribution has been reinforced through modern scholarship (see below, Chapter 2) but remains open to debate in the absence of documentation. Inigo Jones (1573–1652) had pioneered the classical style of architecture in England after travelling in Italy and studying the villas of Andrea Palladio (1508–1580) and meeting his follower Vincenzo Scamozzi (1552–1616). Chevening has a convincing claim to be the earliest, and highly influential, example of this new classicism in British country house design.

What makes Chevening so important as a prototype for the classic country house in the English-speaking world is not only the balanced elevation but also the plan. The floor plans of

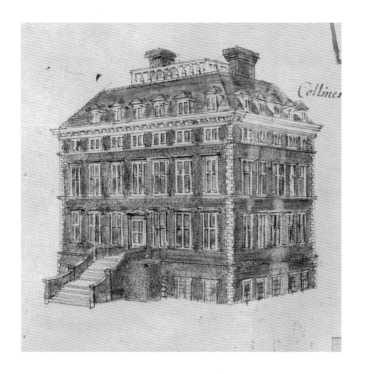

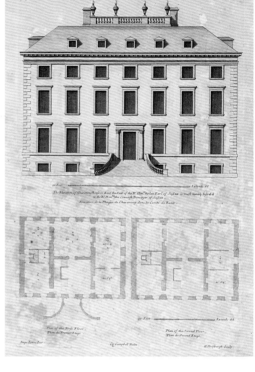

FIG. 6
Chevening, as illustrated in Colen Campbell,
Vitruvius Britannicus, *vol. 2, 1717, engraving*

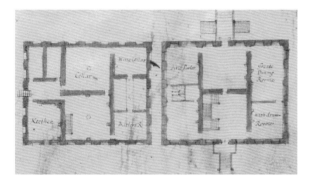

FIGS. 5i, ii
Chevening, details from the estate survey, 1679,
by Richard Browne

Chevening reveal a compact, symmetrical circuit
of rooms of a 'double pile' house, the hall and
saloon set back-to-back in the middle, between
central load-bearing walls, with secondary
rooms to either side. This must have struck early
visitors as a convenient (and warm) innovation,
in contrast to the great hall and extensions of
earlier British country houses, which usually
resulted in H-shaped layouts of rambling rooms.

THE GREAT HALL

Early views and plans reveal that the house had its main entrance on the opposite (south) side to today, and that a substantial architectural staircase filled the left (east) side of the present entrance hall. When Roger North visited his aunt, Lady Dacre (d. 1698), widow of the 13th Lord Dacre, at Chevening he found "the whole is an Italian designe", with "a room of *entrata*, where the great stairs rise to the sumit of the house, and so open to the midle room above". North also found "the staires are too steep". The three flights would have been made of stone with carved wooden balustrades and followed the walls, turning through right angles. When Lady Dacre's son, the 14th Lord Dacre, reorientated the house so that visitors entered from the north, he condemned residents to blasts of cold air surging through the stairwell, as Jones never intended.

The great surprise in Chevening's Great Hall is the replacement staircase, commissioned in 1721 and completed in 1723 (figs. 7, 8 and 9). Swirling upward through three storeys, seemingly without any support, this virtuoso set-piece of engineered carpentry is a unique survival in Britain. In the absence of other documentation as to why, to replace Inigo Jones's staircase, this extravagance was deemed necessary, we can at least imagine Lady Stanhope, only daughter of the nabob 'Diamond' Pitt, widowed at age twenty-nine, pregnant with her second set of twins, looking forward to the day of its completion. She may have imagined herself descending to welcome her guests, wearing a dress of such fashionable width as would have caught on the tight corners of Jones's old carved balustrades. The replacement oak staircase is six feet wide, sufficient to

FIG. 7
The Hall, Chevening, 1888, by George Scharf

accommodate the panniered court dresses of the early eighteenth century.

When Lord Stanhope died in 1721 his young widow was already mother to five children and had been countersigning all the household accounts and the receipts for his salary in their seven years of married life. Lucy Stanhope's husband left a personal estate of around £40,000 and King George I granted her a pension of £2,600 a year. So it was business as usual when, six days after the funeral, Lady Stanhope's father, Thomas Pitt, wrote that "Mr Dubois promises to finish ye stair [up to] all expenditure". Stanhope had admired the one at Dubois's home in Brewer Street, Soho, which no longer survives.

Nicholas Dubois drew on his expertise as a military engineer to create this illusion of a hanging staircase, rising up through two gyrations past one landing before concluding at another. From the top landing there is a thrilling (or vertiginous) view down through a twirling forest of oak handrails, balusters and 56 steps of sweet chestnut (fig. 9). It is subtly supported by cantilever beams, two in the first flight and three in the second, but it still sways, creaks and groans if too many people use it at once. Probably a Huguenot by birth, Dubois had served in Flanders and Spain before retiring from military life in 1713. He provided the English translation for Giacomo Leoni's edition of Palladio's *Four Books of Architecture* (1715–18), a copy of which belonged to Lord Stanhope. Dubois was appointed Master Mason in the government's Office of Works in 1719 and in the 1720s became a developer on Lord Burlington's estate in central London. He would have done more at Chevening but for Thomas Pitt, who decided to employ a different surveyor. We

do not know why Pitt dropped Dubois, but the servants of another client, Henry Pelham, called him "the french son of a Bitch".

The staircase ascends past three full-length portraits (from right to left) – James, 1st Earl Stanhope (artist unknown), King George I (by Godfrey Kneller and his studio) and Thomas Pitt (by John Vanderbank; see frontispiece, p. 2). Pitt stands beside his hat, in which is set the celebrated diamond he purchased in India during his time as the East India Company's Governor of Fort St George in Madras (fig. 10). The huge uncut diamond of 426 carats had been offered by an Indian trader for £100,000 but Pitt paid £20,400. After cutting, in 1717 Pitt sold it to Philippe d'Orléans (Regent of France) for £135,000. As Stanhope purchased Chevening with his wife's dowry that year, we may assume his father-in-law's diamond deal made it all possible (even though Pitt did not receive full payment). After many adventures the 'Regent Diamond' is today in the French Royal Treasury in the Louvre, set in a diadem designed for Empress Eugénie. It is still regarded as the finest diamond in the world.

Another exceptional feature for a British country house completes the ensemble that welcomes visitors into Chevening. The 1727 inventory of the house describes "The Armory" in "the Great Hall looking into the Court". The walls are hung with muskets, bayonets, pistols and swords, all geometrically composed to form decorative trophies (fig. 8). It must have been inspired by the seventeenth-century display in the Guard Chamber at Hampton Court, for there is

FIG. 8
The Great Hall

FIG. 9
The staircase from the second landing

FIG. 10
Thomas Pitt, c.1710, by John Vanderbank

FIG. 11
Lucy Pitt, c.1713, by Sir Godfrey Kneller,
probably painted on her marriage to General Stanhope

nothing comparable from this period in a British country house. The installation may have been designed by the first earl's architect, Thomas Fort, who was Clerk of Works at Hampton Court between 1714 and 1745. The flintlock muskets and pistols were made in Dublin around 1714 for the Antrim Militia, a short-lived corps commanded by Thomas Pitt, Earl of Londonderry, brother of Lucy, Countess Stanhope. The 2nd Earl Stanhope purchased them for Chevening in 1731 for £153. Eighty-eight of the swords may have belonged to the Cinque Ports Volunteers. The centrepiece of the display, indeed of the hall, is the superb armour, made in Milan for the ill-fated commander of the Spanish Armada of 1588, the Duke of Medina Sidonia. It may have been a diplomatic gift to the first earl or his father (see further pp. 85–87).

The hall panelling dates from the late seventeenth century; the Portland stone fireplace was inserted by the first earl and the Portland stone floor would be laid in 1776. Lucy Stanhope did not have long to enjoy the room, for she died in 1723. The furnishing of the entrance hall was completed by her son, Philip, 2nd Earl Stanhope, who invested substantially in the refurbishment of Chevening when he moved in with his twin sister in 1736, aged twenty-one. He commissioned William Bradshaw to provide a suite of gilt furniture for the principal room upstairs on the first floor (see below), and the pair of gilt console tables flanking the front door have probably stood there since that time. The gilt table beneath the stairs was supplied by Bradshaw for the Drawing Room. Against the walls stood a set of eight sturdy mahogany hall chairs, painted with the family coat of arms, also supplied by Bradshaw. These were replaced by the fifth earl with high-backed oak seventeenth-century chairs, but remain elsewhere in the house. The marble busts of the fourth earl and his daughter, Lady Catherine Wilhelmina, both by R. J. Wyatt, were probably begun in Rome in 1834; the latter was exhibited at the Royal Academy four years later (see Chapter 3).

The second earl married in 1745. Navigating the twisting stairs at night must have proved a challenge to Grizel, the second countess, for in 1748 she paid William Hallett for a "Lanthorn stand" (figs. 12 and 13). The lantern itself had hung from the ceiling, as it does once again today (the glass lantern in the stand is a modern replica).

FIG. 12
The stand for the Great Hall lantern, 1748, by William Hallett

FIG. 13
The lantern hanging in the Great Hall

Stained to simulate mahogany, the lantern stand would originally have matched the staircase, which was stripped and bleached in 1973 by the distinguished decorator John Fowler. He also lightened the wall panelling by painting it yellow with shades of white during Chevening's restoration by the conservation architect Donald Insall. Fowler designed the curtains and replaced the stair carpet with the present bordered Brussels.

As well as being Chevening's most memorable interior feature the staircase made a key contribution to the preservation of the house. Chevening is close to the RAF's airfield at Biggin Hill. In the Second World War, but for this staircase, Chevening would have been requisitioned as a military hospital. The creaking, swaying staircase was deemed unsafe for use by stretcher-bearers ferrying the wounded up and down in emergencies.

Five years later Grizel counted everything in the hall, for her inventory (1753, in her handwriting) records "Two Brass Rings for Lanthorns", as well as 161 guns, 364 pistols, 493 swords and bayonets, two shields and the armour. The lantern stand was clearly designed for the centre of the staircase and is an original solution to lighting the upper steps. Negotiating the staircase by hand-held candlelight, stepping through criss-crossing shadows, must have seemed too hazardous. As a type of eighteenth-century furniture, the Chevening lantern-stand is unique. To ensure stability it was carved from a solid trunk of oak, with three legs added.

THE DRAWING ROOM

The present doorway, left of the fireplace, leads to the Drawing Room (fig. 15). In the earliest known floorplan, from 1679, the only doorway in this wall was on the opposite side of the fireplace and led into a withdrawing room, with the 'Great Dining Room' beyond. The third earl used the withdrawing room as a laboratory for his scientific experiments. In 1817–20, after he had inherited in 1816, the fourth earl knocked both rooms together, leaving them connected by a square arch. The present interior trim in the 'Adams' taste (the Victorian revival of the eighteenth-century architects Robert and James Adam) is by William Young and dates from around 1878, complete with a decorative ceiling of *carton pierre* (a form

FIG. 14
*A Gathering in the Drawing Room,
20 August 1859, by George Scharf*

of moulded papier-mâché). Young illustrated his design for this room in his book *Town and Country Mansions and Suburban Houses* (1879). He extended the opening between the two rooms and marked the line of the former dividing wall with a beam and two fluted columns. His colour scheme was white and gold, with two circular overmantel frames (removed 1922). The only visible legacy of the first earl today is the larger chimneypiece, which copies one by John Vanbrugh at Hampton Court. The blue Austrian carpet was unrolled in 1900 over a new parquet floor that had been laid for dancing. A "Grand Ball" for 250 guests was held here in November 1901 (with the orchestra tucked into the alcove) to mark the coming of age of Viscount Mahon, son of the sixth earl. The crimson silk on the walls was introduced by the interior decorator Edward Bulmer (replacing white paint, where Young had intended silk) in 2000, when the paintings were rearranged.

The Drawing Room presents the cream of the Stanhope collection of art. As a country-house collection, Chevening's pictures are unusual in being mostly family portraits. Many of the faces we see were assembled here by the fifth earl, who in 1856 founded the National Portrait Gallery. Some portraits arrived in the twentieth century from the last earl's London townhouse in Eaton Square (the Stanhopes had a succession of different London townhouses). The foundation and core of the collection are the family portraits commissioned by the second earl and his wife, most notably from Allan Ramsay and Thomas Gainsborough (see further Chapter 3).

Visitors are first welcomed by the second earl, as painted by Allan Ramsay (1749). He hangs facing the door from the hall, flanked by later portraits by the same artist of his sons Philip (1762) and Charles (1763; fig. 16). Above them hang Ramsay's portraits of Mary, Lady Hervey (1762), who frequently visited Chevening around the time it was painted, and of Amelia, Lady Lindsay (c.1768), Ramsay's second mother-in-law, who was the sister of the 1st Earl of Mansfield. Prominent as an overmantel is Philip Dormer Stanhope, 4th Earl of Chesterfield (1769; fig. 17) guardian and mentor of the second earl; his portrait was commissioned by the sitter from Thomas Gainsborough in 1769 and presented by Chesterfield to Grizel, 2nd Countess Stanhope. Descriptions of the paintings published for visitors in 1856, 1867 and 1871 record the fifth earl's changing arrangements, when Chesterfield's portrait held pride of place above the chimneypiece in the dining room.

Above the Drawing Room's grander chimneypiece hangs a portrait of William Pitt the Younger, by Gainsborough Dupont (c.1790, fig. 18),

FIG. 15
The Drawing Room

FIG. 16

Portraits in the Drawing Room by Allan Ramsay
of the 2nd Earl, his sons and friends

FIG. 17
Philip, 4th Earl of Chesterfield, 1769,
by Thomas Gainsborough

FIG. 18
The Rt Hon. William Pitt, c.1790,
by Gainsborough Dupont

which was purchased for Chevening in
1845 by Viscount Mahon, ten years before he
succeeded as fifth earl. Pitt's sister Hester married
Charles, the future third earl. Other highlights of
the Drawing Room include Peter Lely's portrait
of Elizabeth, Countess of Chesterfield (c.1661),
purchased by Viscount Mahon in 1842 (see fig. 56),
Pompeo Batoni's portrait of Louisa Grenville (see
fig. 65), who married the 3rd Earl Stanhope (1761)
and Thomas Lawrence's triple sketch of Emilia,
Lady Cahir (1803/04; see fig. 69), the latter two
coming to Chevening through family descent.
This family portrait gallery concludes in the

Dining Room, where the last earl assembled the
Stanhope dynasty.

The Broadwood grand piano was purchased
for the drawing room by the fifth earl in 1865.
Piano music filled the air at Chevening at the
beginning of the nineteenth century, when the
third countess hired a live-in Bohemian music
teacher. However, Mrs Lackner soon played on the
third earl's heart and his countess left him. The last
countess, Eileen Stanhope (see fig. 115), performed
on this piano after dinner to guests; her sheet music
alongside records her love of Mendelssohn, Chopin
and Brahms.

A short wing added by Thomas Fort for the first earl in 1718 provided two small rooms off the Drawing Room on the ground floor. The larger room was originally two closets that were combined by 1866 to form Lady Stanhope's Boudoir (fig. 21). In the smaller room may be seen the estate portrait by Marcus May (fig. 22), which the Chevening trustees commissioned in 2009; another bird's-eye view of Chevening by the same artist hangs in the House of Commons. There also hang here three of the house's collection of fans (fig. 20).

FIG. 19
The West Alcove

FIG. 20
The collection includes several fine examples of eighteenth-century fans; this is French, c.1785, in mother-of-pearl

FIG. 21 (FACING)
Lady Stanhope's Boudoir

FIG. 22
Chevening, 2009, by Marcus May

THE PRINT GALLERY

The theme of portraiture continues into a curving
corridor lined with engravings, many of which
are signed by their sitters as souvenirs of their
visits to Chevening. The Print Gallery (fig. 23)
was arranged by the fifth earl, assisted by George
Scharf, the first director of the National Portrait
Gallery. Early photographs and Scharf's catalogue
of the prints collection (1873) reveal that there
were in total 194 engravings, hung cheek by jowl

(today several are hung elsewhere in the house).
The fifth earl's son and grandson continued the
tradition of asking eminent guests to autograph
their prints or photographs. The celebrities whose
signed portraits may be seen here today include the
Duke of Wellington, Benjamin Disraeli, William
Ewart Gladstone, François Guizot and Florence
Nightingale. The porcelain in cabinets in the Print
Gallery was assembled from around the house by
the fifth earl, and includes a Meissen dessert service

FIG. 23
*The Print Gallery, with armchairs from a suite of
furniture upholstered in Soho tapestry, supplied
by William Bradshaw in 1736*

(c.1800) as well as examples of Worcester, Bow and Chinese porcelain.

William Bradshaw supplied the second earl with a suite of twelve armchairs (six of which are now here) and two sofas upholstered with Soho tapestry in 1736. But for the loss of one sofa and armchair, together with the original case covers and castors mentioned in Bradshaw's invoice, they survive in exceptional condition. The suite originally stood in the 'Carved Room' (now the Dining Room); one armchair was reupholstered for the Library, probably by the fifth earl. In 1869 the windows were hung with "watered crimson stripe French rep", supplied by Howard & Son. The lattice pattern ceiling was designed in 1866 by Lady Mary Stanhope, daughter of the fifth earl. The light fittings date from 1912, when electricity was first introduced to the house.

This gallery forms part of the west wing built by Thomas Fort for the first earl and originally led to the stables. It became more prominent after the library was moved from a room in the centre of the house, at the top of the main stairs, to the upper floor of this wing. The Print Gallery now leads to the library staircase. A selection of maps, documents and a changing display from the collections may be seen in the library vestibule.

FIG. 24
*Thomas Pitt, Earl of Londonderry, c.1720,
by Godfrey Kneller*

THE LIBRARY VESTIBULE

From the Library Vestibule the original staircase of the first earl's western pavilion wing ascends to the Library. The ground floor was built as stables with estate offices and staff accommodation above. The first floor was converted into a library by the fourth earl, with a new coach house below. Following the opening of a new single-storey stable block in

1866, the library was completed by the fifth earl in 1869. The staircase is hung with a portrait of the first earl and two fine full-length portraits that were prominent in the last earl's London town house. Sir Godfrey Kneller's portrait of *Thomas Pitt, Earl of Londonderry* (the first earl's brother in law) was painted around 1720 and still has the kind of frame often found on this artist's portraits (fig. 24). The other full-length, *The Hon. Alexander Stanhope* (father of the first earl), is the masterpiece of John Closterman (see fig. 58). Painted in Madrid in 1698–99, it shows him in Spanish court dress,

FIGS. 25, 26
The Library

and reflects the artist's study of the portraits of Diego Velázquez (as discussed in Chapter 3).

Documents on display in the Library Vestibule include the passport of the Hon. Alexander Stanhope from October 1656, signed *Oliver P*, by the Lord Protector, Oliver Cromwell. As well as painted records of the first earl's battles there is a letter written by Benjamin Franklin (in the third person) to the 3rd Earl Stanhope concerning Lord Chatham's Parliamentary motion for the withdrawal of British troops from Boston, dated January 1775.

THE LIBRARY

The Library of around 17,000 volumes now fills a suite of five rooms (figs. 25 and 26). The first of these comprise the Autograph Room, the Main Library (with the seventh earl's portrait by Sir Oswald Birley, 1936), and the Hansard Room (also known as the Blue Book Room). The fourth earl's instructions to his workmen had specified the reuse of old doors and woodwork and consequently the Georgian panelled doors survive and the windows also retain their original Georgian sash bars. The glazed eighteenth-century bookcases in the Autograph Room may have been installed by the second earl. The main rooms were furnished by the London firm Howard & Son for the fifth earl in 1863–69 and have the relaxed character of a gentleman's club, complete with mahogany chairs upholstered in buttoned red leather (indeed, the Autograph Room is called the 'Smoking Room' in a guide to the house published in 1911). The varnished pine bookcases still retain their original gold-lettered section headings and location references. The Long Library is lined with books on deal shelving fitted by the estate carpenter, with plaster busts of the first and fourth earls and of the Earl of Chatham and William Pitt the Younger. The Long Library leads to the Old Library, devoted to the first earl's books, which form the historic core of the collection. Brought to Chevening by the second earl in the 1730s from his father's house in Whitehall, this core, as recorded in the first catalogue, compiled in 1759, is still intact. Among country house libraries, Chevening's historic collection is one of great distinction, reflecting the scholarly interests, and love of books as books, of generations of the Stanhope family.

The fourth earl catalogued the library in 1817 and moved it to this wing from the main house. The fifth earl (better known as the historian Lord Mahon) completed the suite of rooms, and produced a printed catalogue (1865). He brought important manuscripts to Chevening, many of which are now on deposit in the Kent History and Library Centre at Maidstone.

On 25 July 1769, while living at Chevening for four months, William Pitt, 1st Earl of Chatham (nephew of the 1st Earl Stanhope) wrote to the second earl (then resident in Geneva):

The place is in high beauty, and the plenty of the year more than smiles about us: the fields, according to the sacred poet, laugh and sing. To retire from scenes without – the feast of the eye – to the noble feast of the mind within – your Lordship's admirable library, I have the pleasure to tell you that the books appear in perfect preservation, and speak the commendation of the care which has been taken of that valuable charge. Pitt [Chatham's eldest son, John] was struck with admiration and some fear at the sight of so much learning; but I have relieved his apprehensions by assuring him that he may be the most learned gentleman in England, except Lord Stanhope, if he will read and remember a tenth of the books he sees here.

The library continues to grow to provide recreational reading material of interest to the house's international guests. It is also a place of research. The position of Librarian to the Chevening Trustees is traditionally held by a retired senior member of staff of the National Art Library at the Victoria and Albert Museum.

THE BILLIARD ROOM
The Billiard Room is located off the Print Gallery (fig. 27). Beyond the withdrawing rooms of Victorian country houses, billiard rooms became an essential feature of the male domain, where they doubled as smoking rooms. But billiards has a long tradition at Chevening, as a focus of social life for both sexes. The second earl and his twin sister must have enjoyed billiards with their guests, for in 1737 William Bradshaw was paid for "2 Billiard Tables putt up & Completed in the best

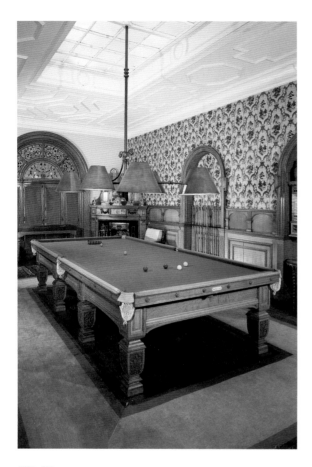

FIG. 27
The Billiard Room

Brampton, wrote to Lady Stanhope: "It was doubted some few days ago that Lord Chat^m was going to have a fit of the gout, but it proved to be nothing but his overtiring himself with playing at Billiards with the young gentlemen and ladies, which occasioned a little pain in his ancle".

In the eighteenth century billiards was also played on the ground floor, in the room opposite the Alcove Room. Under the seventh earl it became his Smoking Room and today it is the house's working kitchen. Billiards moved into the Alcove Room but there was only space for a small table and it was refurnished as a breakfast room in 1869. The new Victorian billiard room required this single-storey extension, which was probably designed for the sixth earl soon after he succeeded in 1875. His architect was William Young, who remodelled the Drawing Room in 1878. Young wrote in his book *Town and Country Mansions and Suburban Houses* (1879) that a billiard room "is a convenient room for guests to pass a wet day, or a quiet evening. Hitherto it has been too exclusively the gentlemen's retreat".

Chevening's Victorian billiard room is a rare, purpose-built, survivor, with its oak table and scoreboard (by Thurston & Co.), raised viewing benches and other fittings still intact. The room only lacks curtains of Turkey red twill, as recorded in 1905, when the Print Gallery had matching curtains. Billiard players can be seen in the decorated tiles in the corner chimneypiece, between scenes of tennis and cricket. This room may have doubled as a garden entrance for sporting guests as it led into a conservatory (built 1885, demolished 1929), which was partly replaced by an arcade (known as the Loggia) facing the parterre.

manner at Chevening". In 1753 the library above the Tapestry Room became the Billiard Room (according to a note left by the fourth earl). The first earl's portrait was hung there in the 1770s. When he lived at Chevening in 1769, Chatham was sixty-one. As a focus of social life billiards proved to be too attractive for a man who had resigned as Prime Minister in 1768 on grounds of ill health. On 20 September 1769 the estate steward, John

THE DINING ROOM

Seven generations of the Stanhope family look down on every diner from their portraits, from the first to the seventh earl, as do several of their wives (fig. 28). The finest are the pair of portraits of the second earl and his wife by Ramsay (1764; see figs. 59, 60), the self-portrait by their son (assisted by J.-E. Liotard) in pastels hung over the chimneypiece (1769; fig. 29) and Gainsborough's portrait of the third earl in his Parliament robe (1786–88; fig. 68).

Originally, when the house faced south, this was the entrance hall. The 1679 plan (see fig. 5) shows doorways next to the entrance front leading to the 'Litle Parlour' (on the east) and to the 'Greate Dining Roome' (to the west). Around 1680 a new entrance hall was created as the house was modified to face north. Roger North, describing Chevening in his treatise 'Of Building' a few years later, noted, "middle backward is a large dining room set off with pilaster and arcuated wainscot". This panelling survives but cannot have been made for the room as it is far from symmetrical, especially on the west wall. The upper panelling may have been moved here from the present entrance hall when the house was reversed around 1680. The dado in the dining room corresponds with the panelling in the entrance hall, so presumably dates from around 1680. The fluted Corinthian pilasters have gilded capitals of moulded lead. The Chevening inventory of 1727 records a "Great Dining Roome" on the floor above, with a "Long Dineing Roome" for the family on the ground floor. At that time the present dining room is described as "The Great Hall going into the Gardens".

FIG. 28
The Dining Room

FIG. 29
Charles Stanhope, Viscount Mahon (later 3rd Earl), Self-portrait holding a portrait of his mother, drawn under the guidance of Jean-Etienne Liotard, 1769, pastel

FIG. 30
A side table in the dining room with a selection from the Silver Trust's collection of contemporary silver

The panelling would have been painted originally but it was grained to resemble oak, with some gilding, probably soon after 1855, when the fifth earl inherited and employed the architect Sydney Smirke to replace the Georgian windows with plate glass and to design "gothic ceilings". The original marble chimneypiece is now in the Alcove Room; it was replaced in the Dining Room by the seventh earl in 1911 with one from Ovenden (the dower house). The panelling was stripped at that time, when the flat areas of oak were added. The lesser-quality timber they replaced indicates that these areas were originally filled by fabric panels.

The strange side tables may be earlier examples of recycling, as they are made out of old window shutters and lengths of carved architectural mouldings featuring fruit, foliage and scallop shells (fig. 30). Like the arch and buffet in the Alcove Room, these fragments are probably all that survives of the original grand staircase. Roger North may have had this in mind when he wrote of Chevening, "There is somewhat of Gothick in the finishing of the rooms, being carved with a sort of grotesque upon the wainscote in the best room below". A visual record of the room dates from 13 September 1859 when George Scharf sketched festivities for the coming of age of Arthur Philip, Viscount Mahon (the future sixth earl), including a *Dance in Dining Room*.

From the Hall, the door opposite the Drawing Room leads into the corridor to the east wing. In the floor plan of the house that illustrates Richard Browne's estate map of 1679 (see fig. 5) the main stairs fills most of the east side of the Hall, with one doorway by the window. The present corridor did not exist and the 'Little Parlour' was entered instead from the present Dining Room. The corridor was created by the fourth earl when he made the Alcove Room around 1817. It is hung with maps of the estate from 1613 (by George Bacheler), 1679 (by Richard Browne), 1705 (by John Brasier) and 1775 (by William Woodward). They reveal how the Tudor house faced south, alongside "The highway from Chepested to London", with another major road, the Pilgrims' Way from Winchester to Canterbury, running across land on the north side of the house. Browne's map features a view of the house as rebuilt in the 1620s, the formal gardens to the south and farm buildings to the north, shielded by high walls, before the division of roads and extensive remodelling of the estate into a landscape garden (as discussed in Chapter 4).

When Roger North visited the Alcove Room was "the comon parlor"; the great parlour was on the other side of the current Dining Room. It became a bedroom in the eighteenth century, then the fourth earl's dining room and then a breakfast room from 1869. The fourth earl inserted the alcove in the north wall for a sideboard, using carved mouldings that may have been recycled from the seventeenth-century staircase and panelling in the present entrance hall. The large pedimented pier-glass is by William Bradshaw, c.1736–37, and was moved from the Drawing Room. The pair of pier glasses now in the Drawing Room date from around 1765 and may have previously hung in the Dining Room. The black marble chimneypiece was designed for the Dining Room by Thomas Fort around 1717, after one by John Vanbrugh at Hampton Court, where Fort was Clerk of Works. It was moved here in 1911 by the seventh earl, who also had the wood carvings bleached. Above it hangs an unattributed portrait of the first earl in a fine architectural frame of the kind made fashionable by William Kent around 1730. The last earl used the Alcove Room as his study and hung here portraits of the wider family.

THE LANDING

The staircase ascends to the principal reception room, which forms the centrepiece of Chevening. The late seventeenth-century panelling continues from the ground floor on to the landing, and surrounds a chimneypiece of Portland stone that was probably designed by Thomas Fort around 1717 (fig. 31). The 1753 inventory records the "Landing place at Tapistry room" as a comfortable setting for taking tea: "Six red Velvet Bottomed Mahogany chairs. A Square japan table, a japan chest. A Square folding mahogany table, a round tee Kettle Stand." The gilded desk-case filled with Stanhope memorabilia has been here since at least 1886; it provides a fascinating diversion from the reception route. Treasures and curiosities include the gold gunpowder horn of Tippoo Sultan, a telescope used by Wellington at Waterloo, and the waistcoat he accidentally left behind after a night at Chevening.

FIG. 31
The first-floor landing

FIG. 32
The Tapestry Room, as arranged for
the Foreign Secretary's meetings

Chevening's finest room could have been even more breathtaking. Two designs by John Webb (1671–72) preserved in the Victoria and Albert Museum (figs. 34 and 35) are all that survive of the "very noble" room he described in 1655, for which Webb was "now making ornaments of wainscott" to complete Chevening for Lord Dacre. As a pupil and assistant of Inigo Jones, Webb conceived an Italianate room that would have resembled his celebrated interiors at Wilton (1648–50). The two drawn elevations, of the north and west wall, reveal that the "very noble" room would have soared up into the next storey of the house, with Corinthian columns or pilasters, paintings set in fitted frames, and sculptural decoration including eagles, reclining figures, swags of fruit and cartouches with an earl's coronet. These two designs also include profiles of ceiling beams that would have continued the detailed cornices into a central square set within eight rectangles. The actual ceiling of this room can be seen in the bedrooms above. The key to identifying these elevations with Chevening is Webb's designs for Corinthian capitals (fig. 33) with paired eagles that match those in the drawings; one is inscribed by Webb: *For ye Eo: Dacres at Chevining in Kent*. However, Webb wrote to another patron in 1655 with regard to Lord Dacre's house: "his roome is very noble & hee bestows much cost upon it, but I am confident yors will be more proportionable".

The project seems to have been abandoned after Lord Dacre went abroad in 1655 "on some discontent between him and his lady". When Roger North visited his aunt, Lady Dacre, he noted, "The cheif room above is not finished, and

FIG. 33
Design for a Corinthian capital for Chevening, c.1655, by John Webb (Royal Institute of British Architects)

was intended to be done with lunetts and small lights *all'Italiana*".

The Tapestry Room we see today is in total contrast to the grand architectural interior that Webb left unfinished (fig. 32). In an inventory from 1723 it is described as the "Great Dancing Room" and four years later the next inventory calls it the "Great Dineing Roome". Webb's Italianate room would have formed the setting for grand receptions and balls. By contrast, the Tapestry Room takes us into a more exotic world. Philip,

FIG. 34
*Design for the west wall of the Noble Room, Chevening,
c.1655, by John Webb* (Victoria and Albert Museum)

FIG. 35
Design for the north wall of the Noble Room, Chevening,
c.1655, by John Webb (Victoria and Albert Museum)

2nd Earl Stanhope and his twin sister Lucy created it in 1736, months after coming of age and moving into Chevening. Abandoning Webb's "very noble" room they took as their starting point the set of tapestries presented to their father in Berlin in 1720 by Friedrich Wilhelm, father of Frederick the Great of Prussia. The tapestries had probably been presented in thanks for negotiating an alliance between Britain and Prussia, but had never been unrolled. They set the height of a new ceiling, the insertion of which formed a new room directly overhead for the first earl's library. Above Thomas Fort's finest chimneypiece, of figured Saravizza marble, Philip and his sister Lucy installed their father's portrait by Balthasar Denner as the overmantel in a fine carved frame, so completing the new room as a tribute to the first earl (fig. 36).

The evidence for this conversion lies in the payments to William Bradshaw, totalling £1,275, to meet his bill of February 1736/37. Bradshaw had the tapestries cut, adjusted and extended in width with "3 borders and two additions" woven in London to fit the room. He also supplied the eight chairs and two settees covered in green Genoa velvet, two pier tables, the fire screen and the curtain cornices, together with the picture frame and ornaments of floral garlands hanging from lion's heads, cornucopiae, laurels and an earl's coronet above the chimneypiece. Bradshaw also supplied the gilt stands for the first earl's lacquer chest and cabinet (fig. 37). Only missing today are the four gilded brackets that would have held small porcelain vases around the portrait of the first earl, as recorded in early photographs. The pair of massive Chinese blue and white shouldered jars, from the Kangxi period (1662–1722), are recorded here in the 1753 inventory; they complement the exotic motifs in the lacquer cabinets and in the hangings. The 1753 inventory also record "Check covers for Hangings in seven pieces. Ditto for all the Chairs & the Screen", which helps explain their excellent condition. Very few eighteenth-century tapestry rooms have survived in British country houses; Chevening's is of exceptional significance as it also retains its original furniture, fully documented, designed to form a complete ensemble.

The tapestries were woven by Huguenot craftsmen from Beauvais who settled in Brandenburg. They are signed by Jean Barraband II (on the left of the doorway) who came from Aubusson in 1686 and ran the tapestry workshop in Berlin from 1708 until his death in 1725. The two tapestries between the windows represent Winter and Spring, after designs by Charles Le Brun (fig. 38). They include the arms of Prussia (a crowned black eagle holding an orb and sceptre) with the initals *FWR* (Fredericus Wilhelmus Rex; see detail p. 6). These medallions were not woven with the tapestry but have been sewn on top; this suggests that this royal gift had been found with some urgency and characteristic economy. Friedrich Wilhelm had dismissed all royal artists and craftsmen when he succeeded his father in 1713 but Barraband's workshop survived on private commissions, until Friedrich Wilhelm could afford to give tapestries as diplomatic gifts.

Flanking the chimneypiece are the other two tapestries from the set of four representing the

FIG. 36
The Tapestry Room chimneypiece,
with the first Earl Stanhope's portrait
by Balthasar Denner, c.1718

seasons. The one to the left has additions to either side of the central motif that are taken from the largest tapestry, on the facing wall. This exotic scene shows acrobats performing on a high wire for a sultan and his lady (shown reclining on sphinx-shaped thrones), whose entertainment also includes Harlequin, Scaramouche, an elephant, a peacock and a camel (fig. 39). This tapestry combines two designs found in Beauvais tapestries made from the 1680s, from a series known as the 'Bérain Grotesques'. Jean Bérain was a designer of masquerades, operas and ballets for Louis XIV of France; his creations spread through engravings. With their plain backgrounds, the 'Bérain Grotesques' had the advantage of being relatively cheap to produce and easily cut up to fit interiors without spoiling their overall design.

Opposite the windows, to the left of the doorway, the signed tapestry represents ballerinas offering flowers to a statue of Pan. The change in colour reveals the extensions supplied by Bradshaw in 1736 to make it fit the room; these sections of London tapestries used weaker dyes and have faded more swiftly. To the right of the door the tapestry represents elegant hunters with hounds, looking for a lion (all on the same marble pavement as in the other tapestries; fig. 40). It has lost the end pavilions equivalent to those in the widest tapestry. Bradshaw also supplied new tapestry for the firescreen and the painted canvas overdoors.

The Tapestry Room was dismantled in 1789 on the orders of 'Citizen' Stanhope, the third earl, who deemed it "too damned aristocratic". It was reinstated in the nineteenth century, probably by the fifth earl, who inherited Chevening in 1855 and employed Sydney Smirke to modernize the windows with plate glass and to design new

FIG. 38
William Bradshaw installed the tapestries and supplied the gilt furniture in 1736

FIG. 37 (FACING)
The first earl's Chinese lacquer cabinet on a stand, 1736, by William Bradshaw, in the Tapestry Room

FIG. 39
*Tapestry, c.1710, showing entertainers before a sultan,
from the 'Bérain Grotesques' series by Jean Barraband II*

FIG. 40
Tapestry, showing hunters pursuing a pair of lions, from the
'Bérain Grotesques' series by Jean Barraband II, c.1710

"gothic ceilings" for this room and the Dining Room. Chevening's tapestries were reinstalled again in 2011 following a five-year conservation programme at the National Trust's Blickling studios, overseen by Linda Parry of the Victoria and Albert Museum on behalf of the trustees.

The white colour-scheme of the room (fig. 32) was chosen by John Fowler in the 1970s, when a fitted carpet replaced one from 1873. William Bradshaw's bill from 1736 does not mention a carpet. The present carpet reproduces an eighteenth-century Axminster at Woburn Abbey, with the addition of a central cartouche representing an earl's coronet and the date it was supplied by D. & S. Bamford, 2005. The conference table (the top in walnut trimmed with ancient bog-oak) was designed and made by Senior & Carmichael in 2006.

THE BEDROOMS

Early inventories (1721, 1723, 1727) describe a suite of formal bedrooms with the "Great Dineing Roome next to the best Bed Chamber" on the first floor. These bedrooms were intended mainly for display and included the "Painted Ceiling Roome" (the State Bedroom, ready for a royal visit, as was the custom), the "Crimson Damask Bed Chamber"; the "Yellow Harriteen Bed Chamber" (harratine is a fabric similar to mohair) and the "Blew Cloth Chamber looking into the Parke". The family's private bedrooms were on the second floor.

Ascending the staircase, today's visitors follow in the footsteps of generations of the Stanhope family. On the second-floor landing the wall cabinets display family souvenirs, including some of the third earl's scientific instruments (such as the calculating machine he invented in 1777, made by James Bullock) and a German toy horse-and-rider given by Queen Victoria to Arthur, eldest son of the fifth earl, on his fourth birthday in 1842.

The central room now facing the second-floor landing would have formed the upper part of the great chamber below, had John Webb's 1655 scheme been completed (figs. 34, 35). An inventory drawn up in 1721 on the death of the first earl records in "Lord Stanhope's Chamber" the only bookcase in the house at that time, with "Bookes: Eighty five Quarto's, Octavo's Twelve Bound and Seventy with Vellom". This room became Lucy, Countess Stanhope's bedroom, or the "Great Middle Room" as described in the inventory drawn up after her death in 1723. By 1727 it was "The Library" (as recorded in the inventory that year) with tables, chairs, two globes and bookshelves (fig. 42). The rest of the first earl's books (1,400 volumes) and bookcases were brought from his house in Whitehall. It then became a billiard room (see above, 'Billiard Room', p. 33), a sitting room and then finally again a bedroom.

In Lady Stanhope's bedroom may be seen the massive ceiling beams of Webb's great chamber; these continue in the adjacent room, which is also above the Tapestry Room. The third earl inserted the partition between 1801 and 1816 so as to divide the larger room into a private sitting room and bedroom. The asymmetry of the beams was probably due to a shortage of timber of sufficient length, while the sag in the beam of the eastern room may be due to the use of unseasoned wood. The beams support an attic but from their size do indeed seem more appropriate to a great central room of two or three storeys. The stone chimneypiece also supports the attic and seems

FIG. 41

*The Chatham Bedroom was furnished to celebrate the family
connection with William Pitt, 1st Earl of Chatham, who lived
at Chevening in 1769, the year after he retired as Prime Minister*

FIG. 42
Lady Stanhope's Bedchamber

too large for the room; it was probably supplied by Thomas Fort around 1717 and, like his other chimneypieces (see 'Landing), was indebted in design to the work of John Vanbrugh at Hampton Court. The house inventory of 1721 also records on this floor two "Great Nurseries". The inventory of 1727 records in the third floor upstairs nine attic rooms, with prints and maps in "Garrett No. 9 otherwise called the Picture Roome".

The fifth and sixth earls furnished the 'Chatham Bedroom' (fig. 41) as a shrine to the Pitt family, with a portrait of John, 2nd Earl of Chatham by George Romney (c.1783–84; first recorded in Chevening in 1904), his younger brother William Pitt's corner washstand (from his official residence at Walmer Castle, Kent) and one of a pair of pier glasses that bears the monogram of Thomas Pitt, Lord Londonderry, who may have inherited it from his father, Governor Pitt.

Most of the historic panelling of the second-floor family bedrooms was removed by the fourth earl soon after his arrival in 1817, when he found his grandfather's flat roof, though it had been tarred, had still failed to keep out the rain. Some

FIG. 43
The Service Wings

panelled doors and chimneypieces survived but the walls had to be re-plastered and hung with paper. The fourth earl also removed the library to its present location, on the first floor of the western pavilion.

THE EAST SERVICE WING

When the 1st Earl Stanhope purchased Chevening in 1717 he found the kitchens located in the high basement of the early seventeenth-century house. One of his first decisions was to build two pavilions, one for the stables (to replace the freestanding building that stood opposite the north entrance) and one for new kitchens and other household services, both with staff accommodation above (fig. 43). While adding to the architectural splendour of the house, the wings had the practical benefit of bringing stabling closer to the new entrance front and of removing the risk of a kitchen fire from the basement. The only inconvenience would have been the smell of the stables and the risk of cold dinners, for his food had further to travel.

After the risk of fire, another reason why the first earl decided to build a service wing with

FIG. 44
The Laundry Room

a great kitchen at its heart must have been his appetite for hospitality (fig. 45). As chief minister to George I he could expect to host and provide banquets fit for a king while also efficiently solving his guests' more prosaic needs, such as clean laundry (fig. 44). Chevening's great kitchen and ancillary rooms were abandoned after the Second World War but remain today as exceptional

survivors from an age when country houses had many servants.

The most vivid and revealing accounts of everyday life at Chevening come from the correspondence of Grizel, Countess Stanhope, wife of the second earl, and the estate's steward, John Brampton, during the countess's absence, when she and the family lived in Geneva between

1764 and 1774 for the health of their sons. Brampton managed the estate of some 3,000 acres with 66 summer staff (including women and children as day-labourers) and eighteen in the winter, in addition to the farm bailiff, gamekeeper and shepherd, who were retained on annual salaries. Their letters cover every aspect of estate management and reveal that the countess was responsible for directing all the steward's actions. They show that she had a remarkable technical knowledge of practical details, from the correct way to stock the ice house from the frozen pond to recipes for soaking bedsteads infested with bugs. Their correspondence also reveals the self-sufficiency of the Chevening estate, from brewing beer in the mansion's brewhouse to farming fish in the lakes.

A curved corridor (fig. 46) links the service wing to the east side of the house, close to the Alcove Room and the Dining Room. Like the Print Gallery, this would have been a plain passageway originally, for busy people marching to and from their domestic offices. Unlike the west corridor, this wing burst into life when meals moved through, as swiftly as possible. The firm wrought-iron handrail to the short staircase was made by Zachariah Gisbourn (who also supplied the forecourt ironwork; see Chapter 2) around 1720 and gave practical support to passing staff. The fine Victorian terrazzo mosaic floor would have smoothed the paths of insulated dinner trolleys. It was probably introduced on the advice of William Young around 1878 when he redecorated

FIG. 45
The Great Kitchen was abandoned after the Second World War but survives intact

the Drawing Room, for he recommended in his book *Town and Country Mansions and Suburban Houses* (1879): "When the staircase is stone, a very beautiful effect can be got by sinking the tops of the steps, and filling them in with mosaic panels. We have a beautiful example of this work in the Museum at South Kensington." Young was referring to the Victoria and Albert Museum, where the building's similar mosaic floors can still be seen.

The two pier glasses carry the monogram of Thomas Pitt and were purchased by the second earl from his uncle. They may have hung first in the main reception room before it was refurbished as the Tapestry Room.

The furnishing of the east corridor as a sculpture gallery dates from the 1970s. The Prince of Wales chose the red wall colour when he had the use of Chevening (1974–80). After busts of the fifth earl and his countess, Emily, by Lawrence MacDonald (carved in Rome in 1854) and of William Pitt the Younger (a copy after Joseph Nollekens), the sculptures terminate with a marble urn commemorating William Pitt, 1st Earl of Chatham (fig. 47). John Bacon carved the Chatham Vase in 1780 for the widow of Pitt the Elder, for their home at Burton Pynsent in Somerset. In 1778 Bacon had won the commission for Chatham's monument in the Guildhall (completed 1782) and in 1779 for his monument in Westminster Abbey (completed 1783). The seventh earl brought the vase to Chevening in 1934 to set it in the gardens. To ensure its preservation, the trustees brought it indoors (fig. 46) and replaced it outside with a replica (see fig. 94).

At the heart of the service wing the Kitchen rises through two storeys (fig. 45). The cavernous

FIG. 46
The East Corridor was redecorated as a sculpture gallery
when the Trustees moved the Chatham Vase indoors

scale of the room allowed heat from the two great oven ranges to escape high over the heads of busy staff. It was last redecorated for the seventh earl in 1912 with the surviving cream and brown colour scheme and giant Stanhope cypher. The Laundry is still fully equipped, with mangle and drying racks from the 1860s (see fig. 44). Furthest away (to be cool) stands the Dairy, lined with blue and white tiles, with its bowls and churns for making butter and cream. The sense of stepping back in time continues in the Butler's Room, Still Room, Bake House, Pantry, Sculleries and Larders. In 1901 there were twenty-four indoor staff including the butler (Arthur Rayner), the housekeeper (Emma Bambrey) and the cook (Emily Clark), with a further fifteen staff for the stables and gardens. Under the trustees, the Brew House has been redecorated for private receptions. The Housekeeper's Room (formerly the Servants' Hall) was refurnished in 2016 as a modern family lounge for the official resident of Chevening. Much of the upper floor has also been refurnished, to provide guest bedrooms. Early inventories record the upper level of the Brew House as the "Dance Room" for staff.

FIG. 47
The Chatham Vase, 1780, by John Bacon

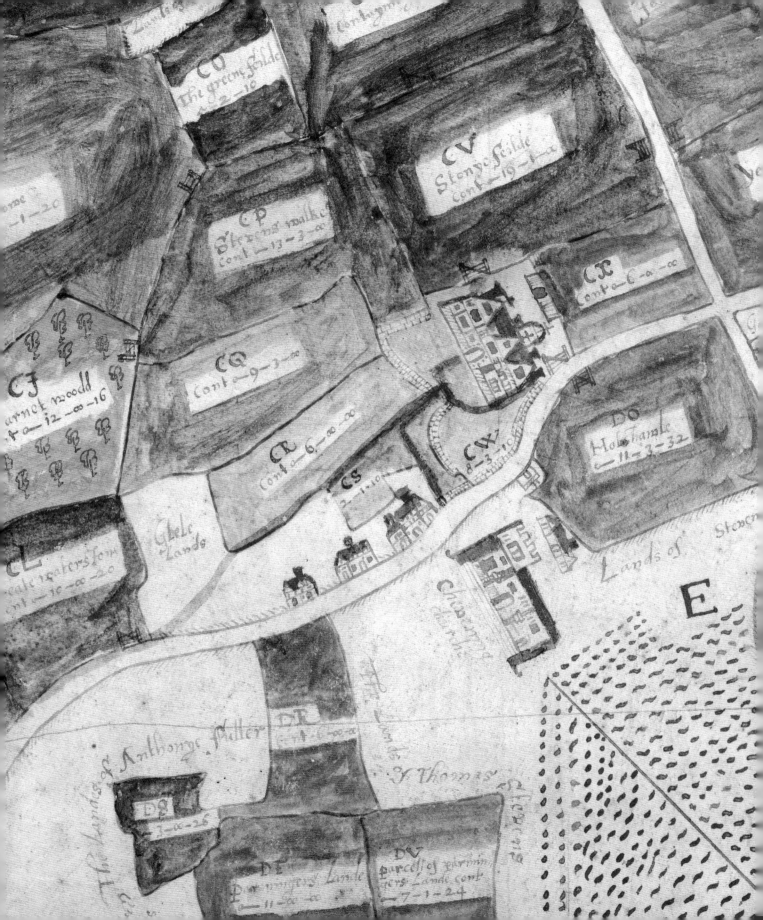

CHAPTER TWO

The Building of Chevening

The earliest documentary records of the Chevening estate date from the turn of the thirteenth century, when Adam de Chevening held the manor, from 1199 to 1216. After several generations, the de Chevening family sold the manor in 1432 to the De La Pole family. In 1551 Chevening was purchased for £420 by John Lennard. In 1604 the Lennards became Lords Dacre of the South by marriage. An estate map drawn up in 1613 by George Bacheler reveals their Elizabethan house, facing south with three gables, a central cupola and a barn, alongside "the highway from Chepested to London" (fig. 48). Today, an outside wall and two mullion windows in the beer cellar (fig. 49) are all that remain visible of the sixteenth-century manor. Part of the fabric survives in the present structure but the rest was demolished by Richard Lennard, 13th Lord Dacre, who inherited in 1616 and married in 1617. Before his death in 1630 he built the compact, classical, red-brick house with stone dressings, seven windows wide and five windows deep, as recorded in Richard Browne's estate map of 1679, both in perspective and in plan (see figs. 51 and 5 above). Above a semi-basement rose three storeys and an attic floor, the plain brick exterior relieved by stone at the corners and around the windows. Another record of the house and estate, by John

FIG. 49
The cellar, with windows from the Tudor house

FIG. 48 (FACING)
A Topographical Plan of the several Manors of Chevening,
Chipstead and Brasted, 1613, by George Bacheler,
detail showing the Tudor mansion house and road to London

Brasier in 1704, shows the entrance gates of the house opposite St Botolph's Church (fig. 50; for the church see Chapter 5).

The traditional attribution of this new house to the architect Inigo Jones was first published by Colen Campbell in the second volume of his *Vitruvius Britannicus* (1717; see fig. 6) along with

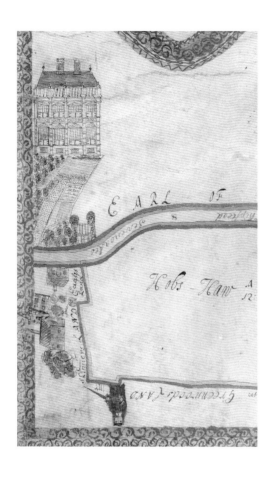

FIG. 50
A Topographical Description of Chevening Warren and other lands, 1704, by John Brasier, detail showing the house, forecourt and entrance gates opposite St Botolph's Church

FIG. 51
A Topographical Plan of the Chevening Estate, 1679, by Richard Browne, detail showing the house and gardens

the elevation, floor plans and Campbell's own proposals for modifying the façade (fig. 52). Research by Professor Andor Gomme, published in 2004–06, leaves little reason to question the attribution, although documentary evidence remains elusive. The floor plans recorded by Browne and Campbell reveal a compact double-pile house (two ranges, back to back), the central spine wall and two transverse load-bearing walls dividing the core into two square reception rooms flanked by a symmetrical group of family and service rooms. Chevening is the earliest known

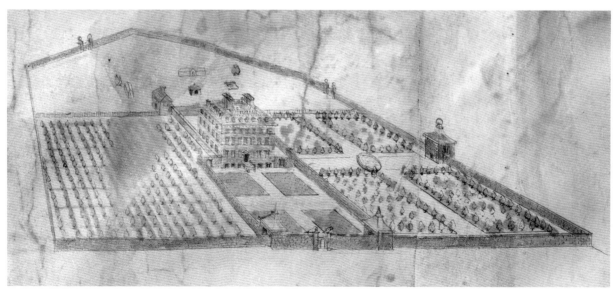

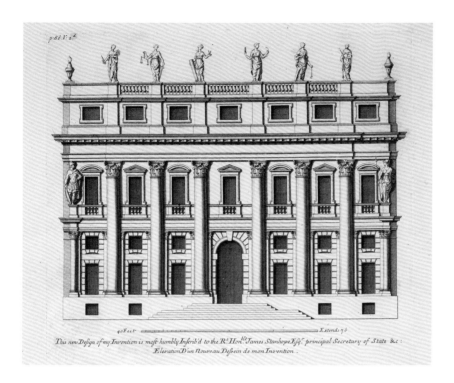

example in Britain of this influential solution to the practicalities of house planning, which Inigo Jones pioneered, on the basis of his study of the sixteenth-century Venetian architecture of Andrea Palladio and Vincenzo Scamozzi. Other indications of Jones as Chevening's architect can be found in the cellars, where classically detailed surrounds to the windows (now doorways) in the east and west walls are indebted in their design to Palladio's book, *I Quattro Libri dell'Architettura* (Venice, 1570), Book IV, p. 94. The cellar vaulting (fig. 49) also resembles Inigo Jones's work in the basements of the Queen's House, Greenwich, and of the Whitehall Banqueting House.

In 1655 the 14th Lord Dacre commissioned John Webb (Inigo Jones's assistant) to create a "very noble" room rising through two storeys at the heart of the house, designs for which survive in the Victoria and Albert Museum (see figs. 34 and 35). These are clearly indebted to that masterpiece of interior design created by Jones and Webb around 1650, the Double Cube Room at Wilton in Wiltshire. However, Chevening's room was left unexecuted or unfinished in 1655, when Lord Dacre decided to live abroad following "some discontent between him and his lady".

Thomas Lennard, 15th Lord Dacre inherited in 1662 and in 1674 married Anne Fitzroy, daughter of Barbara Castlemaine, mistress of Charles II. The main entrance on the south is last recorded in Richard Browne's record drawing from 1679 (fig. 5), which includes brick stacks flanking the external stairs; these imply plans for a grander flight of steps, which was never completed. Around 1680 the main entrance of the house was moved from the south to the north. Despite receiving a dowry of £12,000 when he married the king's illegitimate daughter (who was aged twelve), Dacre, created Earl of Sussex, soon squandered her fortune as well as his own. After shining at the Restoration Court, he died at Chevening in 1715 in debt, without male heirs. After eight generations of Lennard ownership Chevening was sold in June 1717 by Sussex's daughters to General James Stanhope for £28,000.

Stanhope made no substantial changes to the house itself. From 1717 or 1718 he employed Thomas Fort from the Office of Works to extend the house on each side with shallow pedimented wings. These probably provided water closets for the reception rooms and powdering rooms (for dressing wigs) for the principal bedrooms. Fort also added a pair of wings, the west one for the coach house and the east for the kitchen. Connected by curved corridors with blank arches, these colonnaded pavilions form a welcoming forecourt. It is enclosed by a clairvoyée (screen) of elegantly wrought iron work by Zachariah Gisbourn (see figs. 1 and 2) The main entrance, now on the north side, was emphasized in this way but otherwise it remained unaltered from the elevation recorded in 1679, the south and north façades probably being identical.

One reason for Stanhope's respect of the façades may have been Chevening's standing as a house by Inigo Jones. Economy may have been the other reason why Stanhope did not succumb to Campbell's tempting vision, also illustrated in his *Vitruvius Britannicus*, of Chevening as it could look, were he commissioned to modernize it (fig. 52). Campbell described his vision for a palatial upgrading of the main façade by invoking the authority of Palladio:

The Front is richly drest with a large *Corinthian* Colonade of 3/4 Columns, and a lesser Pilastrade of the same Order, to distinguish the two Stories: At the two Angles are 2 small 3/4 Columns, which support a *Mars* and a *Pallas*, as *Palladio* has done in the Palace of *Vilmarana* at *Vicenza*; whose Example I think a sufficient Authority.

Despite Campbell's proposals, the only sculptural enrichment commissioned by Stanhope was from Thomas Fort, who (according to a letter written in 1721) "designed the Figure of a Gladiator standing upon a Pedestal in the middle of the Grass Platt and Military Trophies in the Blank Windows of the Offices". None of these survives. The estate offices were in the new pavilion wings, which face north, each with a rusticated entrance and row of French oeil-de-boeuf attic windows. As these round windows are identical to ones designed by Nicholas Dubois for a house in Hanover Square it is possible that, while creating the circular staircase in the Entrance Hall around 1721, he also designed the wings (which Fort then built).

The main external alterations to Chevening began in 1776–77 when the second earl replaced the hipped roof and dormer windows with a rectangular attic storey beneath a flat roof. The second earl's architect, long misidentified as the fashionable James Wyatt, is unknown. In 1780 Robert (or his brother James) Adam applied his patent oil cement to the exterior. This failed and there were legal consequences (as the Adam brothers also faced when their new product failed at Kenwood). After three lawsuits Adam paid £1,200 in damages. An alternative solution had to be found, as the house was damp. In 1785 Grizel, wife of the second earl, wrote of the state of the building:

… now our porticos are falling, the south one at the salon is propped, the north one at the Hall door has so many props within and without that the passage is shut up …. Should any other part of the House do the same, which I must fear, we shall be in a fine situation, and shall be glad to get back to our quarters in the pigeon-holes in the wing.

When the third earl succeeded the following year, 1786, his first priority was the damp. Between 1786 and 1796 the third earl treated the flat roof with "best Swedish tar" and paper (his own invention) and clad the entire building with dun-coloured "mathematical tiles", which made it look like stone from afar. This building material had been fashionable in Brighton since the 1760s, applied over timber-framed buildings. Examples can be seen in the blank arches of the corridors linking the house with its pavilions; these were left when the tiles on the main house were finally removed in 1970.

To achieve a flat surface for the tiles the stone mullions around the windows and the stone corners of the building were chipped smooth from 1786. In 1788 William Smith was paid for adding Ionic pilasters to the north and south façades. The second earl also replaced the seventeenth-century windows with large sash panes. The fifth earl in turn replaced these Georgian windows with plate glass after he inherited in 1855. Unfortunately, the third earl's treatment of the flat roof failed and damp ran behind the mathematical tiles, rusting the two iron spikes in each one that had been driven direct into the original bricks, making the iron swell until the spikes cracked the brickwork and the stone corners. Chevening's main block continued to deteriorate behind the tiles for well into the twentieth century.

One of the first tasks of the Chevening Trustees was to employ the conservation architects Donald Insall Associates to assess the condition of the house and make recommendations for its repair. Donald Insall recalls finding Chevening "a shattered and derelict relic of the past – a boxy and problematic pile with dingy ceramic tiles falling off like autumn leaves. But full of opportunities! The Trustees had to decide between 'Preservation', which would imply turning the clock back to a particular date in Chevening's past, or 'Conservation', recognizing that the house continues to change but retaining all that was special and of value. The architectural solution to this particular problem had to be a radical one."

After much debate with the Historic Buildings Council (the forerunner of English Heritage), the Georgian Group and other bodies, an extensive programme of conservation was launched. Between 1969 and 1973 Insall's removed the mathematical tiles, replaced much of the shattered red brickwork, created a new hipped roof with dormers and reinstated the small-paned sash windows. The north front was given a central pediment to justify the Ionic pilasters and echo the two pavilions, rather than attempt to recreate the seventeenth-century house (fig. 54). In 1975 the restoration project received a Medal for Scheme of Exceptional Merit in European Architectural Heritage Year (fig. 53). Refaced and restored, the building we admire today is better presented and maintained than at any time in its history. As Donald Insall sums it up, "Now Chevening lives on".

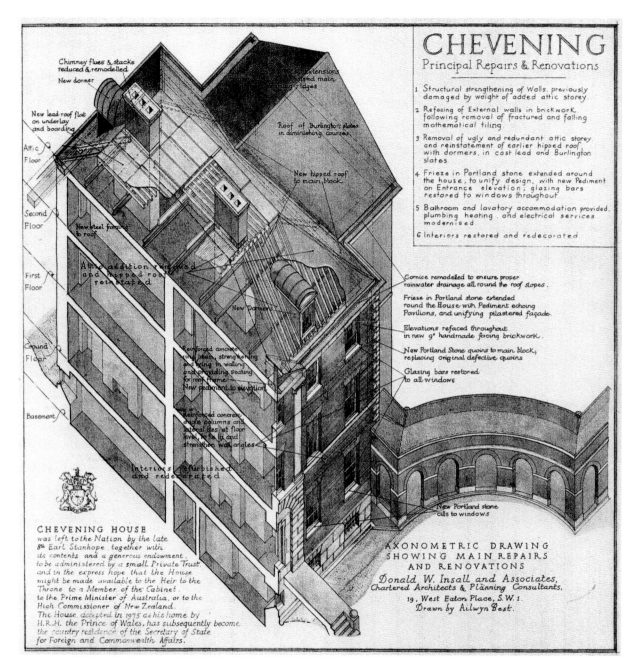

Within the illustration:

CHEVENING
Principal Repairs & Renovations

1 Structural strengthening of Walls, previously damaged by weight of added attic storey.

2 Refacing of External walls in brickwork, following removal of fractured and falling mathematical tiling.

3 Removal of ugly and redundant attic storey, and reinstatement of earlier hipped roof, with dormers, in cast lead and Burlington slates.

4 Frieze in Portland stone extended around the house, to unify design, with new Pediment on Entrance elevation; glazing bars restored to windows throughout.

5 Bathroom and lavatory accommodation provided, plumbing heating, and electrical services modernised.

6 Interiors restored and redecorated.

Chimney flues & stacks reduced & remodelled.

New dormer

New lead roof flat on underlay and boarding

Attic Floor

Second Floor

First Floor

Ground Floor

Basement

New steel framing to roof

Attic addition removed and hipped roof reinstated

New Dormer

Reinforced concrete ring beam, strengthening and tying in walling and providing seating for roof frame

New pediment to elevation

Reinforced concrete angle columns and lateral ties at floor level, to tie in and strengthen wall angles

Interiors refurbished and redecorated

Extensions covered main ridges

Roof of Burlington slates in diminishing courses

New hipped roof to main block

Cornice remodelled to ensure proper rainwater drainage all round the roof slopes.

Frieze in Portland stone extended round the House with Pediment echoing Pavilions, and unifying pilastered façade.

Elevations refaced throughout in new 9" handmade facing brickwork.

New Portland Stone quoins to main block, replacing original defective quoins

Glazing bars restored to all windows

New Portland stone cills to windows

CHEVENING HOUSE was left to the Nation by the late 8th Earl Stanhope, together with its contents and a generous endowment, to be administered by a small Private Trust, and in the express hope that the House might be made available to the Heir to the Throne to a Member of the Cabinet, to the Prime Minister of Australia, or to the High Commissioner of New Zealand. The House, accepted in 1975 as his home by H.R.H. the Prince of Wales, has subsequently become the country residence of the Secretary of State for Foreign and Commonwealth Affairs.

AXONOMETRIC DRAWING SHOWING MAIN REPAIRS AND RENOVATIONS

Donald W. Insall and Associates, Chartered Architects & Planning Consultants, 19, West Eaton Place, S.W.1. Drawn by Ailwyn Best.

FIG. 53

Chevening: Principal Repairs and Renovations, 1975, by Ailwyn Best for Donald W. Insall and Associates

FIG. 54
Chevening, the entrance front today

FIG. 55
Chevening, the entrance front in 1969,
prior to restoration

ELIZABETH COUNTESS OF CHESTERFIELD.
SIR PETER LELY.

CHAPTER THREE

The Collections

The most obvious distinction of the Chevening collection today is the exceptional quantity and variety of good family portraits. A visitor is never alone when looking around the rooms, for there are eyes everywhere. It is unusual to find a country house collection confined to portraits by leading painters, especially when so many are still in their fine historic carved and gilt frames and have supporting documents in the Stanhope archives. Chevening lacks the usual dark old masters of doubtful attribution, of classical landscapes, mythological subjects and sea-pieces, bought by some extravagant ancestor in Italy as a gullible youth on the Grand Tour. Also absent are any hunting scenes set on the estate, with portraits of favourite horses and dogs, which the same patrons usually came to prefer once back home.

A visitor might first assume that this collection of portraits is the result of ancestor gathering by Philip Henry, 5th Earl Stanhope, the distinguished historian who, in 1857, founded the National Portrait Gallery (NPG). In this, and in the original arrangement of the paintings, as a family portrait gallery, Lord Stanhope had the assistance of George Scharf, first director of the NPG, who was a regular house guest at Chevening. Scharf can be found in a group photograph with the sixth

FIG. 57
George Scharf (second from left) with the 6th Earl Stanhope (far right) and friends at Chevening, August 1877

FIG. 56 (FACING)
Elizabeth, Countess of Chesterfield, c.1661, by Peter Lely

earl taken in 1877 (fig. 57). This group is standing outside the Print Gallery, which Scharf helped to create (see Chapter 1). Scharf's contribution to Chevening also lies in his 33-page catalogue of this gallery of prints, handwritten in 1873, and in his own charming drawings that record and evoke family life in the house and wider estate (see figs. 7, 14, 90–92, 103).

Clearly, Scharf was excellent company for he turns up as a frequent guest at other country houses, including Knole and Madresfield. He published catalogues of the paintings at Blenheim Palace (1862), Knowsley Hall (1875) and Woburn Abbey (1877, 1890) as well as for the Society of Antiquaries (1865) and the NPG itself, so it is surprising that he did not produce a catalogue for Chevening. However, a modestly titled *List of Portraits and Busts in the Principal Rooms in Chevening* was published anonymously by the fifth earl in 1856, a year after he inherited (revised 1867, 1871, 1931), and in this Scharf must have had a hand. The fifth earl brought furniture and portrait busts to Chevening from his townhouse in Grosvenor Place, Mayfair, in 1856. He arranged the main family portraits in the Dining Room, gathered the ones by Ramsay in the Drawing Room, and hung the wider family relations in his study, the Alcove Room. In his commitment to portraiture the fifth earl built on a great Stanhope family tradition.

The first earl's father, the Hon. Alexander Stanhope, gazes down from his splendid full-length portrait now hanging over the Library staircase (fig. 58). The masterpiece of John Closterman, it shows Stanhope in black Spanish court dress as the English Resident in Madrid, painted in the manner of Velázquez. As recorded in a series of letters between the sitter and his son, of 1698–99, in the family archive, James Stanhope took the artist to Madrid as his patron, to meet his father, as a first stop before Rome. The sitter wrote to his son in November 1698, referring to the gorget-like collar of court dress, "Mr Cloysterman is drawing me at length in Golilla with other Spanish ornaments; it will be a very good piece, and I hope serve to introduce him where I cannot go myself, for his ambition is to make the Queen's picture". Alexander Stanhope's portrait succeeded in attracting commissions for portraits of Charles II of Spain and of his queen, Marie d'Orléans, before Closterman went on to Rome. By way of thanks, the artist presented this portrait to James Stanhope in April 1699. The portrait's location seems modest today but in 1856 it hung in the Drawing Room, with three other full-lengths, of Governor Pitt, of the first earl (both now on the main stairs in the Hall; see frontispiece and fig. 10) and of Thomas Pitt, Earl of Londonderry (also now over the Library stairs; see fig. 24). This stately group of gentlemen must have been broken up when the Drawing Room was remodelled in1878.

The Scottish painter Allan Ramsay became this country's most fashionable portraitist of the mid eighteenth century, before Reynolds and Gainsborough. A close friend and regular guest of the second earl and his family, Ramsay visited Chevening with his wife even while the second earl and his family were away in Geneva. Ramsay painted portraits of the second earl (1749; 1764), of his Scottish countess, Grizel (1764), their eldest son (1749, 1763) and second son (1764), all of which are at Chevening (see figs. 59–63), with three other portraits by the same artist. Chevening has the largest group of family portraits by Ramsay, even though the fifth earl gave three more away, to the Earl of Haddington (see below).

The range of Ramsay's repertoire can be seen at Chevening by comparing the family's commissions

FIG. 58
The Hon. Alexander Stanhope, 1698–99, by John Closterman

FIG. 59
Philip, 2nd Earl Stanhope, 1764, by Allan Ramsay

FIG. 60
Grizel, Countess Stanhope, 1764, by Allan Ramsay

over two decades. They range from the informal outdoor portraits of the second earl, who seems lost in a dream (see fig. 108), and of his infant son sitting on the lawn with his drum from the same year (1749; fig. 63), to the portrait of Anne, Countess Temple (1760), seated in profile before a neoclassical chimneypiece and table (fig. 64). Ramsay knew the second earl well enough to describe his twenty-year old heir, in 1773, as "deficient in manners of dress and modes of behaviour requisite in mixed company ... which, however trifling they may seem to scholars, are very essential in life". Viscount Mahon may have polished his social skills, for in August 1782

Ramsay thanked the second countess for "such agreeable company (which I prefer to every other)". Ramsay was declining her invitation to stay at Chevening, even though "your ladyship is so good as to make your house to be to me as like my own as possible".

It seems likely that the Countess, the Scottish-born Grizel, initiated the commissions from Ramsay, as her brother, the 7th Earl of Haddington, was one of his earliest patrons. In the year of her marriage, 1745, Grizel commissioned a set of nine intimate portraits modelled in wax relief by Isaac Gosset. They represent herself, her husband, her grandparents, mother, aunt and sister,

FIG. 61
Charles, later 3rd Earl Stanhope, 1763, by Allan Ramsay

FIG. 62
Philip, Viscount Mahon, 1763, by Allan Ramsay

along with Philip, 4th Earl of Chesterfield, who was her husband's cousin, principal guardian and mentor. Grizel would have been introduced to Gosset by Ramsay, for the Huguenot craftsman was also the painter's supplier of picture frames. Typical of Ramsay's choice are the Rococo frames on the pair of portraits of Philip and Charles Stanhope. A more classical type of frame favoured by Ramsay and Gosset and still united with its original painting can be seen around the portrait of Anne, Countess Temple; it is a 'Carlo Maratta' type (named after the seventeenth-century Italian painter) with its distinctive rows of acanthus leaves.

The finest carved Rococo frame surrounds Sir Peter Lely's portrait of Elizabeth, Countess of Chesterfield (fig. 56). This portrait was probably painted to mark her marriage to Philip, 2nd Earl of Chesterfield; she died four years later. Horace Walpole hung it in his Great North Bedchamber at his Gothick villa in Twickenham, Strawberry Hill, and may have commissioned the superb gilt frame, which appears to date from around 1755–60. Philip, Viscount Mahon, later 5th Earl Stanhope, purchased it at the Strawberry Hill auction in 1842.

Another outstanding Rococo frame surrounds another masterpiece, Pompeo Batoni's portrait

FIG. 63
Philip, Viscount Mahon, 1749, by Allan Ramsay

FIG. 64 (FACING)
Anne, Countess Temple, 1760, by Allan Ramsay

In November 1769 Grizel wrote to Hester, Countess of Chatham (her cousin by marriage) hoping her husband would "do me the honour and pleasure of sitting for his picture for Chevening". Chatham made Chevening his home for four months in 1769 after retiring as Prime Minister. The Stanhope and Chatham families were twice linked through marriage. The 1st Earl Stanhope married Lucy Pitt, heiress daughter of 'Diamond' Pitt, grandfather of Chatham, and the third earl married Chatham's daughter, Lady Hester Pitt. Chatham's portrait at Chevening was painted in 1772 by Richard Brompton (fig. 66). On 12 October 1772 Grizel wrote to the Countess of Chatham: "To begin with the picture – I can't tell you how pleased we all are to hear it is so like, and how obliged for the patience in contributing so much to the making it so".

On 7 December 1769 Grizel wrote of her success in persuading her husband's mentor and former guardian, Philip Dormer Stanhope, 4th Earl of Chesterfield, to sit for his portrait (see fig. 17). Despite his being deaf and infirm at age seventy-six he consented to having his likeness taken by "Gainsborough at Bath, which is, I hear extremely like; it will be sent to Chevening". Chesterfield had served as ambassador to The Hague, as Lord Lieutenant of Ireland and as Secretary of State but is best known for his letters to his natural son, Philip Stanhope, who held diplomatic posts in Hamburg and Dresden before his death aged

of Louisa Grenville, later 3rd Countess Stanhope (fig. 65). Her uncle, Richard, 3rd Earl Temple, commissioned this portrait in November 1761 when she was aged three and in Rome. Travelling with her parents, Louisa and her terrier puppy were on their way to Constantinople, following the appointment of her father, the Hon. Henry Grenville, as ambassador to the Ottoman Empire. Batoni records her in her first semi-adult dress (perhaps a purchase in Rome). The frame would have been carved in England after the portrait arrived from Rome and is exceptional in presenting a wreath of leaves, fronds or feathers, tied at the top with a string of pearls. The portrait probably came to Chevening soon after her marriage in 1781 to Charles, Viscount Mahon, later 3rd Earl Stanhope.

thirty-six. The letters were begun in 1737 and
first published in 1774, a year after Chesterfield's
death. Dr Johnson's verdict, that "they teach the
morals of a whore, and the manners of a dancing
master", did not take into account their purpose.
Chesterfield's *Letters* provided a Machiavellian
course of instruction for an illegitimate young
man making his career in society, preferably as
an international diplomat. They continue to be a
bestseller today, in many foreign languages.

Gainsborough's definitive portrait of
Chesterfield in old age hung over the chimneypiece
in the Dining Room by 1856 and now hangs as an
overmantel in the Drawing Room, paired with a
portrait of Chatham's second son, William Pitt
the Younger, as the other overmantel (see fig. 18).
Painted by Gainsborough Dupont, nephew
and assistant of the master, Pitt the Younger's
portrait was purchased by the fifth earl (when

FIG. 68
*Charles, 3rd Earl Stanhope, 1786–88,
by Thomas Gainsborough*

Viscount Mahon) in 1845. The third earl followed his mother's example and commissioned his own portrait from Gainsborough shortly after he succeeded in 1786 (fig. 68). Gainsborough's receipt for part payment of this 60-guinea portrait is preserved in the Stanhope papers. Unlike most of the last works painted before the artist died in 1788 it was not completed by Gainsborough Dupont; the peer's robe appears to have been left unfinished at the artist's death.

The fifth earl's commitment to collecting probably began in 1842, when, at the Strawberry Hill auction (as Viscount Mahon), he purchased the magnificent portrait by Peter Lely of Elizabeth, Countess of Chesterfield, second wife

of Philip, 2nd Earl of Chesterfield (see fig. 56). He bid again at the Stowe sale in 1848, when he purchased William Hoare's portrait of the 4th Earl of Chesterfield (1742). At the same auction he purchased Thomas Hudson's portrait of Hester Grenville (painted in 1750, four years before her marriage to the Earl of Chatham; fig. 67) and Hudson's portrait of John, Earl Grenville (1742).

When Gustav Waagen, director of the Royal Gallery in Berlin, published his great three-volume survey *Treasures of Art in Great Britain* in 1854 (the year before the fifth earl inherited) he did not include Chevening, nor did it feature in his supplementary volume, published in 1857, which covers a further forty British collections. This fourth volume does, however, describe two paintings hung "as companions in the library of Lord Stanhope's town residence" in London. They were a three-quarter-length portrait of Philip II of Spain ("one of the best of the portraits of this monarch by Titian. Bought by Lord Mahon in 1844") and a portrait by Velázquez, previously identified as of the Count-Duke of Olivares, "formerly in the collection of Count Lecchi at Brescia, and purchased thence by Lord Stanhope – then Lord Mahon – in 1846". In 1857 Stanhope lent his Titian to the 'Art Treasures of England' exhibition in Manchester; in 1861 he lent both his Titian and his Velázquez to the 'Old Masters' exhibition at the British Institution and in 1888 he lent both to the 'Art Treasures' exhibition in Leeds. When the seventh earl published a new edition of the *List of Portraits* in 1931 he recorded the Velázquez hanging over the dining-room chimneypiece in his townhouse, 111 Eaton Square, but did not mention the Titian, as he had sold it at Christie's in 1928. Both portraits await rediscovery.

As well as his purchases, the fifth earl sought donations of other family portraits while weeding the collection of some wider relatives. In 1860 the third earl's portrait of Benjamin Franklin, painted by David Martin, returned from the sitter's family, to whom it had been left by the third earl in 1817. The fifth earl gave three portraits by Allan Ramsay from Chevening to the Earl of Haddington for his house at Mellerstain; his generosity denuded the largest private collection of portraits by Ramsay. He also commissioned copies of portraits he could not acquire. In 1845 an artist named Gooderson copied a portrait of Sir Michael Stanhope (d. 1552), great-grandfather of the 1st Earl of Chesterfield. In 1847 Gooderson painted a copy of a portrait of Catherine Grey, Countess of Hertford (1538–1568) and her son, from the original at Petworth, and in 1855 the same artist copied a portrait of Anne Stanhope, Duchess of Somerset (1497–1587) from the original at Syon House.

Several portraits arrived at Chevening through inheritance. Batoni's portrait of Louisa Grenville (see fig. 65) was commissioned by her uncle Richard, 2nd Earl Temple; he probably left it to her on his death in 1779 and it would have come to Chevening in 1781 on her marriage to the future third earl. Rivalling the Lely as the most glamorous painting at Chevening is Thomas Lawrence's unfinished triple portrait of Emilia, Lady Cahir (fig. 69), which descended through her family to Evelyn, wife of the sixth earl. Lawrence performed with Lady Cahir at a private theatrical country house party and told his sister that Lady Cahir was "so beautiful, that I felt love-making very easy". The triple oil sketch is inscribed *Painted by Thomas Lawrence in a fit of folly*, presumably when they withdrew during the house party.

After Viscount Mahon succeeded as fifth earl in 1855 he encouraged appreciation of the collection by publishing, in 1856, a room-by-room *List of Portraits*, describing fifty paintings and ten busts; new editions appeared in 1867, 1871 and 1931. Comparison reveals how the arrangement changed in his day, most notably in the Drawing Room (see Chapter 1). Growing recognition of the collection's importance is evident from the loans made from Chevening to exhibitions. In 1866 the fifth earl lent Lely's *Countess of Chesterfield* to the first 'Exhibition of National Portraits' held at the South Kensington Museum (today the Victoria and Albert Museum). The following year he lent to the second in this chronological series four of his best paintings – *Chesterfield* by Gainsborough; *1st Earl of Chatham* by Brompton; *3rd Earl Stanhope* by Gainsborough, and *Lady Hester Grenville, afterwards Countess of Chatham*, by Hudson.

The fourth earl is not recorded as a collector but he must have supported a campaign of conservation of the paintings undertaken (perhaps by his son, Lord Mahon) in 1848. The archives preserve from 30 October 1848 an amusing letter of thanks, supposedly signed by the portrait of the Earl of Chatham and other paintings:

> We the undersigned Family Portraits entreat you to accept our grateful thanks for the care and kindness which you have shown in attending with so much assiduity … to our cleanliness and personal appearance. We looked as if our Linen were soiled, as if our faces and hands had not been washed, as if our clouths were dirty and dusty, so that were unfit to be seen, and ashamed to shew ourselves. We have now become under your continual

EMILY COUNTESS OF GLENGALL
1775 - 1836
SIR T LAWRENCE

FIG. 69
Emilia, Lady Cahir, later Countess of Glengall,
1803 or 1804, by Thomas Lawrence

superintendence, and by the indefatigable exertions of Mr Hearth so neat and spruce that we could attend a Levee or a Drawing Room. We have observed with great satisfaction that Governor Pitt has a new pair of Diamond Buckles, and that he has now the comfort of standing by an open window from whence he enjoys a view of the sea and of some picturesque rocks on the shore. We are much rejoiced to find that the Honourable Alexander Stanhope has been resuscitated, although he was for a time covered with Paper, like a Winding Sheet, and remained invisible which gave us serious apprehensions for his fate, and we are credibly informed that the holes in his garments will be repaired with the same skill as would be done by Mr Paine who is known to be a first rate Tailor. We are however under some uneasiness that the smell of Varnish may have had an injurious effect on Lady Temple and Lady Lincoln who appear by their complexions to have delicate compositions, and we would respectfully recommend to you to perfume them some of the fragrant essences which may be procured in great perfection from Hendrie in Tichbourne Street.

Busts were also commissioned and collected and complement the paintings. In 1833 Lord Farnborough presented the future fifth earl with an original plaster bust of Pitt the Younger by Francis Chantrey. The marble busts of Philip, 4th Earl Stanhope and his daughter, both by R.J. Wyatt, were begun in Rome in 1834; Lady Catherine Wilhelmina's bust was exhibited at the Royal Academy in 1838. The pair of marble busts of the fifth earl and his wife were carved in Rome in 1854 by Lawrence MacDonald. In 1845 a bust was cast from Rysbrack's monument to the first earl in Westminster Abbey by "Mr Scouler" for Lord Mahon. This was probably William Scoular, who was appointed Sculptor in Ordinary to the Duke and Duchess of Clarence in 1823. Scoular may have also made the marble bust of Chatham, which was copied from one sold at Stowe in 1848 to Sir Robert Peel. A bust of Pitt the Younger (copied by *W.M.* after Joseph Nollekens) was acquired for the entrance hall in 1904. The last earl also brought to Chevening John Bacon's commemorative marble urn to William Pitt, 1st Earl of Chatham, which had been commissioned by Chatham's widow in 1780 (see fig. 47). The most beautiful sculpture at Chevening is the monument by Chantrey to Frederica Stanhope (1827), sister-in-law of the fourth earl, in St Botolph's Church, at the main entrance to the estate (see Chapter 5).

The seventh earl continued the family commitment to collecting portraits through purchase, commissioning artists and through inheritance. In 1901 he inherited from Catherine Wilhelmina, Duchess of Cleveland, sister of the fifth earl, the self-portrait pastel of Charles Stanhope, Viscount Mahon aged sixteen (fig. 29). He is shown holding his portrait of his mother Grizel, Countess Stanhope, having set aside his volume of Euclid (while his cricket bat and ball stand ready). It was drawn in Geneva in 1769 under the guidance of Jean-Etienne Liotard. Another rare artist for a British country house collection is Antoine Prud'Homme, whose portrait of the same sitter five years later (signed and dated *Preudhome pinxit/1774)*, shows Viscount Mahon in uniform as Commander of the Geneva Archers Company, with the city of Geneva in the background (fig. 70).

FIG. 70
Charles Stanhope, Viscount Mahon (later
3rd Earl), 1774, by Antoine Prud'Homme

The seventh earl purchased in 1901 a pastel of the third earl, inscribed on the reverse *Painted by Ozias Humphrey at Chevening House 1795*. In 1939, when Geoffrey Dawson, editor of *The Times* and a prominent 'Empire Loyalist', offered more portraits, the last earl declined, writing that he was only buying "direct ancestors". The seventh earl commissioned the leading conservator Horace Buttery to carry out two campaigns of cleaning, in 1924–39 and 1947–55. Today there are more portraits at Chevening than ever before; early twentieth-century photograph albums reveal portraits now in the house that were formerly on display in the last earl's London townhouse.

While fine portraits are the most obvious characteristic of the art collections at Chevening, the other distinction among country house contents is the early Georgian library. After the historian Thomas Macaulay visited Chevening he wrote to the 5th Earl Stanhope that the library "has a unique interest as an example of what were the books of an English gentleman". The first earl's library remains the core of the collection, but the Chevening library also reflects the intellectual interests of later generations. The second earl was a Greek scholar and a noted mathematician. The third earl patented several of his mechanical inventions, and the fifth earl was a well-published historian.

The first earl's library of over 1,600 volumes was valued on his death in 1721 at £350 (his annual salary as chief minister to King George I had been £1,200). To the 400 books inherited from his father he added many of his own, collecting from 1717, initially as a practical aid to his career as a diplomat. Having spent much of his military career in poorly funded campaigns in Spain and its Mediterranean colonies he preferred the pursuit of peace through negotiation rather than conflict, and spent much of his political career travelling to Paris, Berlin, Madrid, Vienna and, with King George I, to Hanover. The first earl's skills as a linguist are reflected in the number of books in the Library in other languages (he was fluent in German and Spanish) including Latin (348 titles), French (192) and Italian (119). Arthur Onslow, Speaker of the House of Commons, wrote that "He was the best scholar of any gentleman of his time .... He had studied long and knew more the affairs of Europe [sic]". His love of books came from his father, the Hon. Alexander Stanhope, King William III's envoy to Madrid, from where he wrote to his son in 1696:

> I have picked up some good Greek books, and am glad to hear by Mr Jerrick they may still be of use to you, though in Polybius [which] he says you read this winter you found nothing comparable among the old Greeks or Carthaginians or Romans to what you have seen and out-done already in your short time.

Highlights of the first earl's collection include volumes acquired in Spain in 1690. These have richly tooled bindings of Italian or Spanish crimson morocco with armorial stamps, which reveal them to be from the library of the 1st Duke of Medina de los Torres, Viceroy of Naples. Despite sales since 1920 (when *Country Life* devoted a long article to the library), eighteen examples remain, published between 1541 and 1634, including C. Wytfliet, *Descriptionis Ptolemaicae augmentum* (Louvain, 1597). Each book has the Duke's stamp impressed in the front board and that of his second wife, Anna Caraffa, Princess of Stigliano, on the

FIG. 71
Etymologicon magnum *by Friedrich Sylburg (Heidelberg, 1594), as bound for the 1st Duke of Medina de los Torres, c.1630*

FIG. 72
Robert Simson, Apollonii Pergaei Locorum planorum libri II *(Glasgow, 1749), in a mid-18th-century Scottish binding*

rear board (fig. 71). The earliest book in the library is *Enee Silvii Senensis rerum familiarium epistole*, by Aeneas Silvius Piccolomini (Pope Pius II), published in Nuremburg in 1481. The earliest book on gardening still at Chevening is Charles Etienne, *De re hortensi* (Paris 1536), which is signed on one of the flyleaves 'Jhon Leonarde', by John Lennard, who purchased the estate in 1551.

Contemporary books owned by the first earl include the second volume of Colen Campbell's *Vitruvius Britannicus* (1717), which features Chevening (see figs. 6 and 52), and Giacomo Leoni's edition of *The Architecture of A. Palladio in Four Books* (1715). The first earl is listed among the subscribers

to Campbell's second volume. Stanhope and his wife also collected practical books on horticulture, such as the edition of La Quintinie's *The Complete Gard'ner* by George London and Henry Wise (1717).

The second earl inherited his father's love of books and trebled the library in size. A distinguished mathematician, he sponsored the publication of the works of Robert Simson in 1768, and owned a copy of Simson's *Apollonii Pergaei Locorum planorum libri II* (Glasgow, 1749; fig. 72), with a contemporary red morocco binding. The early scientific, mathematical and astronomical books reflect the intellectual interests of the second and third earls, and include Euclid, *Liber*

FIG. 73

Jean-François Marmontel, Poëtique Françoise *(Paris, 1763), as bound for Marie Adelaïde, daughter of Louis XV of France*

elementorum in artem geometricae (Venice, 1482), and three by Isaac Newton – *Principia* (1687), *Philosophiae naturalis mathematica* (London, 1687) and *Opticks* (London, 1704). Several manuscript pages of scientific diagrams dating from the early fifteenth century were found inside one volume in 1997. The fourth earl probably acquired the volumes with fine French bindings such as Marmontel's *Poëtique Françoise* (Paris, 1763; fig. 73) which belonged to Marie Adelaïde, daughter of Louis XV. There is also a presentation copy of Charles Darwin's *Origin of Species* (London, 1859), given by the author, who lived nearby at Downe in Kent.

Having begun his military training aged nineteen, General James Stanhope did not have the advantage of a Grand Tour with its opportunities to collect classical sculpture and Old Master paintings, but he did acquire thirteen Roman tombstones. They were presented to him in 1708 by the Mayor of Tarragona in thanks for his military services as Commander in Chief in Spain, and are preserved within the garden shelter known as 'Fort Mahon' (see fig. 85). The best known of the altar tomb inscriptions is *FACTIONIS VENETAE FVSCO* … – to the charioteer Fuscus from the Blue team. We can still read the praises of the sportsman's devoted fans from the second century AD, recorded on the tombstone in Latin: 'Your reputation is unsullied, you won fame for speed, you contended with many, though not rich you feared nobody, though you experienced envy you always bravely maintained silence'. It ends in Greek: 'The ages will talk of your contests'.

The fine princely armour that forms the centrepiece of the Great Hall (figs. 74 and 75) may also have been a diplomatic gift, either to General Stanhope or to his father, the ambassador to Spain. It was made around 1588 by Pompeo della Cesa or by an associated armourer in his workshop in the Castello Sforzesco in Milan (unfortunately the breastplate on which he usually placed his signature has been replaced). From his monogram (combining the letters C, O [NDE], N, I, E, B, L, A), which recurs ten times on the armour, its first owner was identified in 2017 as the commander of the Spanish Armada in 1588, the Duke of Medina Sidonia, Count of Niebla. The fine etched decoration mimics fashionable embroidery. The armour is not mentioned in the 1723 inventory of Chevening; in her inventory of 1753, Grizel, 2nd Countess

Stanhope, notes only "A Suit of Armour, with a long sword in one hand & Mr Stanhopes Spontoon in the other". The spontoon (a pike) is also recorded by George Scharf in his drawing of the stairwell from 1888 (see fig. 7). An account of Chevening published in 1886 describes it as "inlaid with gold" at that time; originally it would have been black with gold highlights.

Medallions commemorating the achievements of the first earl in the course of his military career also survive in the collection. The gold medallion showing Stanhope killing the Spanish general in hand-to-hand combat on horseback at the Battle of Almenara in 1710 (by John Croker; fig. 76) is the source for one of four marble medallions on his monument in Westminster Abbey, by William Kent and Michael Rysbrack. The Trustees purchased a pair of designs for this monument (figs. 77 and 78), which was commissioned after the death of Lucy, Countess Stanhope in 1723, in accordance with her will, and was unveiled in 1733.

The year the monument to his father was unveiled the second earl was in Italy. A British resident minister there wrote to the Earl of Essex, "… he likes neither painting statuary nor architecture: and takes no delight in these things which take up all the time of most other young men …. He has read a good deal of Divinity, Metaphysicks, and Mathematicks." He did, however, make one major acquisition while abroad. On the advice of the painter Allan Ramsay, he purchased a manuscript in Geneva; years later he donated it to the British Museum, as his wife Grizel wrote to Lady Chatham in 1765:

Lord Stanhope has made a present to the museum of a very valuable piece of antiquity;

FIGS. 74, 75
Research for this book in 2017 revealed that the armour forming the centrepiece of the Great Hall had been made for the Duke of Medina Sidonia, commander of the Spanish Armada of 1588; the armour is Milanese, attributed to Pompeo della Cesa

FIG. 76
Gold and silver medals struck to commemorate the Battle of Almenara, July 1710, designed by John Croker, showing General Stanhope killing the Spanish general

that he "had the happiness of his country so much at heart, that he had neglected his own, and left little else to his son but the honour of having a seat among their Lordships". However, thanks to the second earl's trustees (including Chesterfield) by the time he came of age the family's finances enabled him to invest in the furnishing of Chevening.

One of his trustees, Thomas Pitt, Earl of Londonderry, had lived at Chevening while the second earl grew up in Geneva; he left some of his furniture and collection in the house when he moved out. In 1735 the second earl purchased, for £153 17s 3½d, the arms he then arranged as trophies on the staircase. He paid Londonderry a further £293 7s 8d for furniture, which included two mirrors with Londonderry's monogram, *T.P.* In July 1736 the young earl commissioned William Bradshaw to make furniture, with payments of £200 and £1,000 on account for the set of gilt furniture in the Tapestry Room (two settees and eight chairs). Bradshaw also supplied two settees and twelve armchairs upholstered with Soho tapestry. The same month the second earl paid the silversmith Paul de Lamerie £605.

The second earl's most enduring contribution to the display of Chevening's collections was his installation of the set of tapestries presented to his father by Friedrich Wilhelm, father of Frederick the Great of Prussia in 1720 (see Chapter 1). Once again the second earl turned to William Bradshaw. The Chinese lacquered cabinet and chest in the Tapestry Room had probably belonged to the first earl, and they were mounted on gilt stands as part of this tribute installation (see fig. 46). Two lacquered tables from around 1710 may also reflect the first earl's taste.

the original articles of Magna Carta, presented by the Barons to King John; as such a thing might be lost in private hands, he purchased it to place it in safety.

The British Museum sent a letter of thanks on 26 May 1769 for the gift of the original draft of Magna Carta, a facsimile of which hangs in the library vestibule.

The first earl left no great fortune for his widow and heirs to spend on furnishing Chevening. His son's guardian, Philip Stanhope, 4th Earl of Chesterfield, told the House of Lords in 1734

FIG. 77

Design for the monument in Westminster Abbey to James,
1st Earl Stanhope, c.1727, by Michael Rysbrack

FIG. 78

Design for the monument in Westminster Abbey to James,
1st Earl Stanhope, c.1727, by Michael Rysbrack and William Kent

The Georgian family silver is one of Chevening's great losses. In 1759 the second earl offered "four thousand ounces of my silver plate to be sent to the Mint", for melting down as coinage to support the cost of warfare, but there is no evidence that his offer was taken up. However, we know from the fourth earl's detailed list, with weights in ounces, what his father sold. It begins with a note of silver weighing 7,166 ounces in total in the possession of the first earl at his death, which included silver "received by grant from George I 30 August 1717". The Chevening house sale held by Sotheby's on 10 May 1993 included 124 lots of silver, among a total of 811 lots. In 2014, given the absence of fine silverware for formal display at events, the trustees negotiated the transfer from 10 Downing Street to Chevening of a loan collection of contemporary British silver commissioned by The Silver Trust (see fig. 30).

CHAPTER FOUR

The Park and Estate

Chevening enjoys an idyllic rural setting (figs. 79 and 80), disturbed today only by the distant thunder of the orbital road around Greater London's outer reaches. One would hardly guess that the M25 is less than a mile away. But this cherished sense of privacy came at a price. Approaching the estate along Chevening Road, the village ends abruptly at a gate between the churchyard and a high brick wall. This was once the main road to London and continued north to meet the ancient Pilgrim's Way that ran from west to east, just 350 yards north of the house, until both roads were diverted in 1786 by the third earl. After he laid out a better road (at his own expense) further south the village became a quiet hamlet at the estate gate. Sadly, the main fresh fish trade no longer passes the house on its way from Hastings and Rye to London; the Stanhope Arms inn and the shops opposite the church closed long ago.

The classic English landscape garden we find at Chevening today is largely the creation of the fourth earl, who succeeded in 1816. His daughter, Wilhelmina, wrote in her manuscript memoirs:

FIGS. 79 AND 80 (OVERLEAF)
A picturesque footpath encircles the canal to the south and 'Chatham's Ride' sweeps through the escarpment to the north.

He was an expert woodsman …. He had made Chevening what it was. He found it a house standing in a hayfield, when he first came, and he surrounded it on two sides with beautiful Italian gardens of his own design, and a broad green lawn sloping down to the piece of water called the Canal. All the flowers and shrubs were hardy, and of these he had a vast collection, for he never came home without bringing seeds from abroad …. The shrubberies and pleasure grounds were also laid out by him, with a maze something like the one at Hampton Court.

The fourth earl so loved Chevening that he even added a codicil to his will, warning his heirs and successors that

Having during many years and much expenditure greatly improved and adorned the gardens, the pleasure ground, parks and woods of the family mansion at Chevening, it is my most solemn injunction to every person who may hereafter possess the same to leave unaltered the sight and arrangement of the said gardens, pleasure grounds, parks, woods and plantations and to preserve and cherish all my said works … to be perpetuated to future ages.

FIG. 81
*Detail of the estate survey by Richard Browne, 1679,
showing the entrance close to St Botolph's Church*

The fourth earl may have found the estate so neglected by his eccentric father that it resembled "a hayfield" but there lay structure beneath, on which he built through extensive planting. The earliest known estate map, drawn by George Bacheler in 1613 (see fig. 48), shows the Elizabethan manor house by the road with just a stable block standing on the north side. An estate map drawn by Richard Browne in 1679 for the then owner, Thomas, 15th Lord Dacre, includes three views of the new Italianate house, set within a walled garden; one view shows the start of a southern avenue and the river before it became a lake (fig. 81). After 1688, when Dacre separated from his wife, Anne Fitzroy (illegitimate daughter of Charles II and Barbara Castlemaine), he began

laying out formal gardens around the central lake. His vision may be behind the engraving published in 1719 after a drawing by Thomas Badeslade in the first volume of John Harris's *The History of Kent* (fig. 82). This bird's-eye view reveals a great formal garden stretching south of the house, its geometric structure consisting of an axial central thermometer-shaped canal linked by diagonal allées to wide bordering avenues, framed on the left (east) by a high wall along Chevening Road and to the right by planting with pasture for grazing deer beyond. Within this framework winding paths lead through a 'wilderness' and to a mount. The 'keyhole' in the screen of trees on the crest of the North Downs may have been first cut around this time; echoing the canal in shape, it provides a point of reference for the north-south axis running through the estate and gardens (figs. 3, 4).

The engraved view by Badeslade does not simply present a new patron's aspirations, for it is confirmed by a detailed topographical survey made around 1720 (fig. 83). This plan reveals a ha-ha (concealed trench) running down the west side to keep the grazing livestock at bay. It also features a wide avenue of trees on the north side as the first earl's new approach to the house from the Pilgrim's Way across the North Downs. Books still in the library at Chevening, such as Stephen Switzer's *Iconographia Rustica* (1718) and John Laurence's *The Clergy-Man's Recreation: Shewing the Pleasure and Profit of the Art of Gardening* (fifth edition, 1717) may indicate that the 1st Earl Stanhope took a hands-on approach. Badeslade's aerial prospect also resembles a plan for a rural and forest garden published by Switzer in *Iconographia Rustica*. Moreover, various characteristic features in the garden suggest the advice of the king's

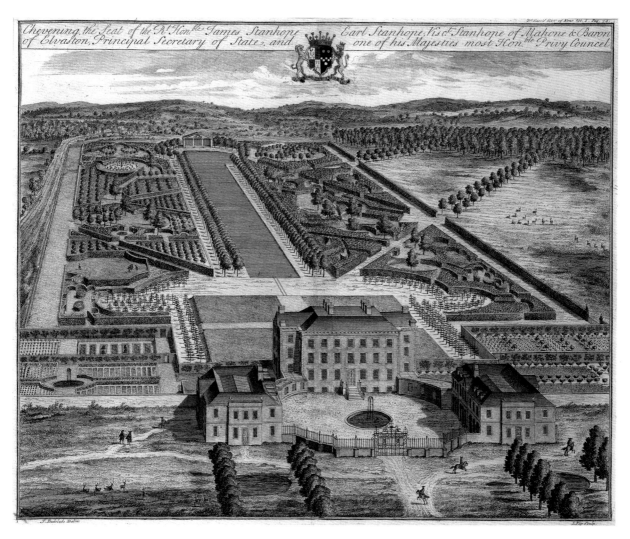

Chevening, the Seat of the R.t Hon.ble James Stanhope Earl Stanhope, Visc.t Stanhope of Mahone & Baron of Elvaston, Principal Secretary of State, and one of his Majesties most Hon.ble Privy Councel

T. Badeslade Delin: I. Kip Sculp.

FIG. 82
Aerial view of Chevening by Thomas Badeslade,
1719, engraved by Johannes Kip

landscape designer, Charles Bridgeman. This garden predates Alexander Pope's influential garden at Twickenham and Charles Bridgeman's designs for Stowe. However, it seems unlikely that the garden existed fully as drawn by Badeslade, for the 1st Earl Stanhope only purchased three acres at the southern end of the canal in 1718, the year after he acquired Chevening. He must have planned to entertain out of doors, for the inventory drawn

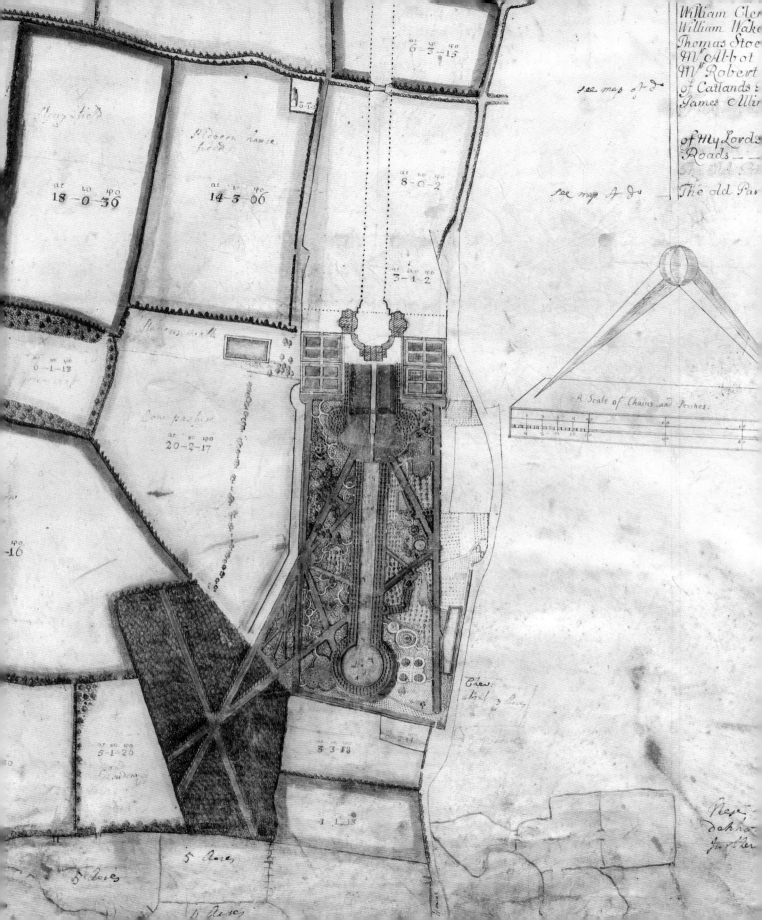

William Cle...
William Wake...
Thomas Stoe...
Mr Abbot
Mr Robert
of Catlands
James Ulm...

of My Lords
Roads

The Old Par...

see map of do

see map of do

Clay field
at. 10. 40
18 – 0 – 30

Pidgeon house
field
at. 10. 40
14 – 3 – 06

at. 10. 40
6 – 3 – 15

at. 10. 40
8 – 0 – 2

at. 10. 40
3 – 1 – 2

at. 10. 40
6 – 1 – 13
green croft

Stones walk

Cow pasture
at. 10. 40
20 – 2 – 17

40
–16

at. 10. 40
5 – 1 – 26
the meadow

3 – 3 – 13

Chev
about 3 acres

4 – 1 – 13

5 Acres

5 Acres

5 Acres

A Scale of Chains and Perches.

Nesse
doth not
further

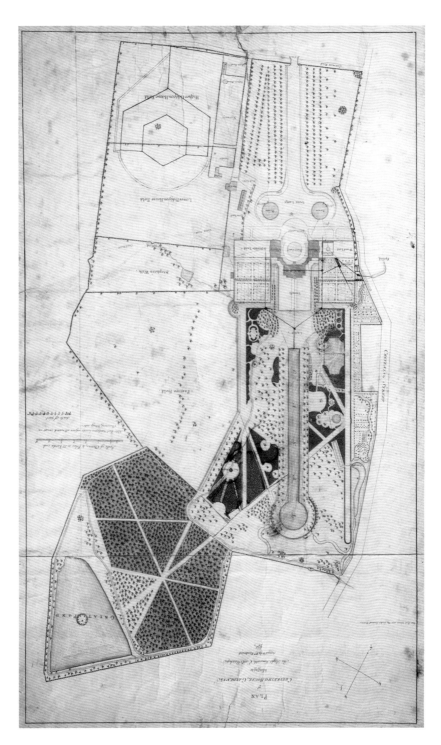

FIG. 84
Estate survey by William Woodward, 1775

FIG. 83 (FACING)
Estate survey, c.1720, detail; the drive to the north
of the house continued to 'the keyhole' and beyond

up after the death of his widow in 1723 includes "Thirty four large Garden Seats, 60 Windsor chairs painted Green".

The building accounts for 1776–78 record how Grizel, Countess Stanhope oversaw the creation of a new kitchen garden, which she removed from the east and west sides of the house. It survives today, north-west of the house, its double hexagon of brick walls designed to ensure that fruit could grow in the sun on each side of the eight-acre garden, the outer walls providing a buffer against frost. Grizel's meticulous accounts reveal the range of her stock of plants that supplied all the needs of the kitchen and house, from vegetables and colourful sweet-smelling cut flowers to melons, grapes and figs. One must imagine the house and garden full of flowers when Grizel lived here, for, as she wrote to her steward in March 1773:

I hope to find a great many flowers up and down, I can never get half enough Hollyhocks, Sun flowers, White Lillies, Stocks &c which cost little money & [are] little trouble & make a great show when dispersed. I would have Lilly of the Valley at the low HaHa where the Laurels are to be planted, it grows very well there, & in short a vast many flowers, sweet sorts & showy ones that are not so.

Another survey, drawn by William Woodward in 1775 (fig. 84), records this hexagonal kitchen garden. 'Fort Mahon' (fig. 85) is also clearly marked, west of the canal, housing the first earl's collection of Roman tombstones. This survey reveals how Grizel and her husband remodelled the gardens after the second earl's income increased following his inheritance of estates in Devonshire and Ireland (in 1765) and in Derbyshire and Buckinghamshire (in 1773). The canal was widened to resemble a natural lake, with islands (fig. 86). Fed from the hills, it flows into the River Darent. The 'keyhole' was also re-cut in the woods on the summit of Madamscot Hill, north of the house.

A romantic carriage drive through the estate, 'Chatham's Ride', was created at the suggestion of the Earl of Chatham, who lived here in 1769. On 6 September 1769 the estate steward, John Brampton, wrote to Lady Stanhope in Geneva that Lord Chatham "has desired a Bridle road, or for a Carriage, to be opened for him from the white gates above the Bridge … which will come out in the Sundrish road … it will be about a mile to come to the London road … he thinks when it is done it will be the pleasantest ride he ever saw." Writing on 18 October 1769, Chatham promised Stanhope, "I venture to pronounce, that the approach from the London side to Chevening … the most beautiful approach in any place in England". Today, visitors discover the house from the east side, with some surprise, thanks to Chatham's taste for the picturesque. Grizel did not take up his suggestion that they commission Lancelot 'Capability' Brown to remodel the entire parkland as a landscape garden.

When the third earl moved the public roads and raised the brick wall that divides the estate from the village, soon after he inherited in 1786, he may have sought not only greater privacy and

FIG. 85
The collection of Roman tombstones installed as the garden feature 'Fort Mahon' was presented to General James Stanhope by the mayor of Tarragona in 1708

FIG. 86
*Alongside the canal sit the historic boat house
and (more recent) bathing jetty*

security but actual secrecy. A scientific inventor, the third earl showed less interest in the park than his parents but he did use the lake, albeit as a test-tank. There he tried out steam-driven paddle boats for naval use, and experimented with methods of defence against floating mines, conscripting his family and staff as his crew (see Chapter 6).

The fourth earl, having fled from his father, returned to Chevening from Germany on inheriting in 1816, but his claim that he found "a house standing in a hayfield" was clearly some exaggeration. He was angry at his father's neglect of the gardens but the comment may say more about his own preference for formality over the English picturesque aesthetic. As well as extensive planting of specimen trees, the fourth earl introduced the lawn that slopes down to the south and west of the house; he planted the hornbeam allées and extended the winding gravel paths in the pleasure grounds around the lake (fig. 87).

FIG. 87
A fine prospect from the south front of the house

An amateur botanist, the fourth earl was related through his mother to Sir Joseph Banks (first director of the Royal Botanical Gardens, Kew) and a founder member of the Medico-Botanical Society of London. He planned two 'Italian' parterre gardens on the south front and around 1820 he planted the maze (fig. 88). A plan at Chevening is annotated *Labyrinth into Chevening Gardens laid out by the 4th Earl Stanhope 1820 from a plan left* [by] *his grandfather the 2nd Earl.*

The fifth earl inherited in 1855 and must have immediately commissioned a new plan for the pair of Italianate parterres, one on each side of the garden steps, for it is inscribed *Summer of 1855*. He also commissioned designs for the Kitchen Garden and for the Summer House Wood. The maze was replanted after the Second World War by the seventh earl, who also added the Flower Garden. The lower pair of parterres reverted to lawn in the 1970s but survive in photographs.

FIG. 88
The 'labyrinth' was designed by the second earl
and planted in around 1820 by the fourth earl

In August 1867 J. L. Motley (American ambassador, 1869–70) wrote of his memorable weekend at Chevening:

The gardens were a blaze of glory. I had never seen them in their full magnificence before, and such roses and such profusion of them it was never my lot to see. I enjoyed the velvety turf, the verdurous groves, the weird looking yews, the luxurious house, and I cannot wonder that those born to such things wish … to rest and be thankful.

Scharf's drawings are evidence of the enjoyment that the guests took in the grounds at the time of the fifth earl – drives and picnics, celebrations and tenants' dinners (figs. 90–92).

A letter to Evelyn, the sixth countess (framed in the Library vestibule) records another happy guest. On 31 July 1911 Archibald, 5th Earl Rosebery (Prime Minister 1894–95, and nephew of the fifth earl) scored through the heading on the printed stationery 'Chevening Sevenoaks' just one word: "Paradise". There could be no higher praise, but one weekend a regular guest, Rudyard Kipling,

FIG. 89
A loggia overlooks the parterre on the south-west side of the house

FIG. 90 (OVERLEAF)
A Picnic at Brasted, 19 August 1870, by George Scharf

Bracted Park G.S. 19th August 1870.

Ly Stanhope.   Genl Hankey   Ld Stanhope   Ld Walden

L. Mahon   M. Cheney?   L. Stanhope   L. Mahon
                        L. Walden

wrote out at Chevening his poem 'The Way Through the Woods' (fig. 93). Tradition holds that the poem was inspired by a stroll at Chevening, perhaps along the Old Rye Road as it runs up the escarpment of the Downs. However, the manuscript is dated 19 October 1930 and Kipling had published the poem in his book *Rewards and Fairies* (1910).

Since the 1970s Chevening's Board of Trustees has invested in the restoration of the gardens, through the expert advice of Elizabeth Banks, George Carter and Marian Boswall. The overall aim is to retain the structure as recorded in 1719, of the central canal, with clear vistas for the allées and cross rides, but as modified as romantic parkland around a picturesque stretch of water. To mark the 300th anniversary of Lord Stanhope's purchase of the estate and fifty years of the Chevening Trust, the cascade was recreated on the south-east side of the canal in 2017.

Today the Chevening estate consists of some 3,000 acres, mostly between the Darent Valley to the east and Westerham to the west, and between a line north of the crest of the North Downs and the M25 motorway to the south. It is actively managed by the Board of Trustees and their agents to generate the income necessary for the upkeep of the house, garden and park. In addition there are nearly 500 acres of managed woodland. The remainder of the estate is tenanted dairy and arable farmland. A number of businesses also operate as tenants in former farm buildings. The Victorian apple store (fig. 95) and bee house (fig. 96) are rare survivors. In addition to Chevening village itself there are more than forty houses and cottages on the estate, which are let out as residential property. All profits are reinvested in the estate.

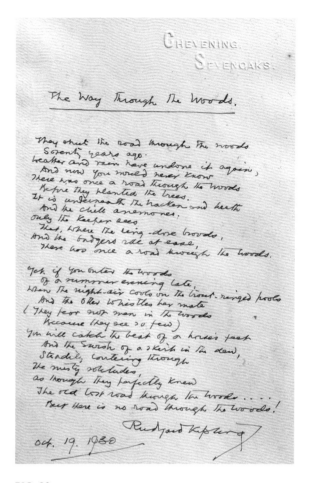

FIG. 93
'The Way Through the Woods', 9 October 1930, manuscript of his poem by Rudyard Kipling

FIG. 91 (FACING, ABOVE)
The Coming of Age of A.P., Lord Mahon, 18 September 1859, by George Scharf – a party for the twenty-first birthday of Arthur Philip Stanhope, Viscount Mahon, later 6th Earl Stanhope

FIG. 92 (FACING, BELOW)
Tenants' Dinner in Honour of the Birth of Lord Mahon, 25 August 1881, by George Scharf – a celebration of the arrival of the sixth earl's son and heir, in 1880, ten years after the birth of his eldest sister

FIG. 95
The apple store is a rare survivor of a Bunyard fruit room,
invented in 1883 as a way to preserve fruit through the winter
and spring in Britain

FIG. 96
The Victorian bee house is home to four hives

FIG. 94 (FACING)
The Chatham vase, a replica made to replace the original
when the sculpture was moved indoors (see figs. 46, 47)

CHAPTER FIVE

The Church of St Botolph

The patron saint of travellers, St Botolph gives his name to the village church (fig. 97). The church is first recorded in 1115; the oldest surviving part is the south aisle, built in the late 12th century, and the tower was begun soon after 1518. It stands close to the Pilgrim's Way from Winchester to Canterbury and the current route passes through the churchyard. This route predates the church and ran east-west along the North Downs, close to the north front of the house. It was moved in 1786 to join the Greenway, the track that today runs east from the churchyard. At the same time the 3rd Earl Stanhope moved the entrance gates to Chevening from opposite the west end of the church to the north, so closing the public road.

The chantry on the south side of the church was probably added in 1584 or 1585 on the death of Elizabeth Lennard, and would have been funded by her family, who owned Chevening at that time. The Lennards became Lords Dacre of the South by marriage in 1604 and owned Chevening for eight generations. The vault beneath this family chantry contains the coffins of the Dacres, together with the mortal remains of the Stanhopes, from the first to the fifth earl and countess. The last two generations of the Stanhope family lie buried in the churchyard (fig. 98). Beyond a low railing, their two rows of headstones face across a terraced and hedged lawn towards the tall monument to the sixth earl, which was erected with subscriptions from the parish (fig. 99). This solemn composition of the Stanhope plot forms a complement to the chantry.

The Stanhope family's commitment to the church is first associated with the peal of six bells that, tradition holds, were donated by the first earl. Four of these had to be sold in 1938 to pay for structural repairs. The oak choir-stalls, rector's stall and matching stall opposite date from 1855 and were funded by the fifth earl (in the year he inherited Chevening) and by his neighbour at Chipstead Place, Frederick Perkins. Following an outbreak of dry rot the church was restored by the sixth earl in 1901–02 with W.D. Caroë, first architect to the Ecclesiastical Commissioners (the sixth earl was First Ecclesiastical Commissioner, responsible for all the Church of England's buildings and investments). Caroë designed the altar rail and oak pews and reconstructed the pulpit using Jacobean panelling.

FIG. 97

The Church of St Botolph, where eight generations of the Stanhope family lie buried in the vault and churchyard

111

FIG. 98
The Stanhope plot in the churchyard

The screen to the chantry was inserted in 1902 by the sixth earl, whose 'S' and coronet mark the entrance. Here in the Stanhope Chantry (as it is traditionally known) can be seen a fine group of sculptural monuments that reflect the fortunes of the owners of Chevening; all are now in the care of the estate trustees. They range from a relatively modest monumental brass with shield and inscription to John Lennard (d. 1555) to the altar tomb of his son, the Lincoln's Inn barrister John Lennard (d. 1591), High Sheriff of Kent. He is dressed in armour, with his wife, Elizabeth (d. 1585), lying on a mat (his head on a bolster, hers on a pillow), both carved in alabaster. His son, Sampson Lennard (d. 1615) led a life of extravagance that continued after his death with the splendour of his funeral and this magnificent monument. His wife Margaret, Lady Dacre (d. 1611) is shown recumbent alongside her husband in alabaster (with her dog at her feet) on a high tomb-chest flanked by black marble obelisks beneath a canopy arch, with their eight surviving children kneeling in rows below (fig. 100). Lady Dacre and her husband lie buried beneath the tomb with their great-grandson (d. 1662) and his son, the Earl of Sussex (d.1715).

Two years after Sussex's death his family sold Chevening to General James Stanhope (d. 1721). He is commemorated by a more modest black marble memorial tablet on the south wall which records how his *consummate talents and glorious services both as a warrior and as a statesman commanded the veneration of his own country and the applause of other nations.* Opposite is a monument erected by Grizel, Dowager Countess, to her late husband Philip and to his grandfather, the Hon. Alexander Stanhope, who was interred in the family vault at Chevening even though he had died ten years before his son purchased the estate. Below, a white marble tablet to the third earl, the inventor 'Citizen' Stanhope, is signed by the sculptor Joseph Kendrick. The inscription was composed by the 1st Lord Holland: *He was endowed with great powers of mind, which he devoted zealously and disinterestedly to political and general science, to the diffusion of knowledge, and to the extension of civil and religious liberty. He requested, by his will, to be buried 'as a very poor man'.*

A black marble slab commemorates the 4th Earl Stanhope and his countess. A pair of wall tablets to the fifth earl and his wife flank the one to the first earl. A tablet on the east wall commemorates the last earl's younger brother, the *Brave, eager* Dick Stanhope, who was killed by a German sniper during the Battle of the Somme on 15 September 1916. Plaques to the memory of the third earl's daughter, the traveller Lady Hester Stanhope, are more recent additions.

These sober Stanhope memorials are outshone by a masterpiece of British neoclassical sculpture from the age of Romanticism, Francis Chantrey's

FIG. 99
The memorial to the sixth earl, raised by public subscription

memorial to Lady Frederica Louisa Stanhope (fig. 101). She married Colonel the Hon. James Stanhope, younger brother of the fourth earl, in 1820 but died in childbirth in 1823, aged twenty-two. She is shown asleep on a couch in her nightgown with her sleeping baby son alongside. The monument was completed in 1827 (at a cost of £1,608), but her husband never saw it erected. The eldest daughter of the 3rd Earl of Mansfield, Frederica Murray had been married at the Mansfield home, Kenwood near Highgate. After her death James Stanhope lived

FIG. 100
The canopy tomb to Sampson Lennard (d.1615)
and his wife Lady Dacre (d.1611) in the chantry

at Kenwood with the Mansfield family, who took care of his surviving son. However, he continued to suffer from a wound incurred at the siege of San Sebastian in Spain, 1813 (a musket ball remained in his shoulder) and, two years after the loss of his wife, he was found hanging in one of the outbuildings at Kenwood. Despite taking his own life he is interred in the same tomb, as recorded in a small inscription on the reverse side of his wife's monument. Lady Frederica Stanhope is also commemorated among the church's handsome collection of ten emblazoned hatchments from Stanhope funerals. These hung over the entrance to the family home during each funeral and were moved to the church at the end of each period of mourning.

A watercolour by George Scharf records the Stanhope Chantry in 1880, with its stained-glass windows and curtained entrance from the churchyard (fig. 103). Five of the church's stained-glass windows were destroyed in the Second World War; only the one in the south wall of the

FIG. 101
Memorial to Lady Frederica Louisa Stanhope, 1827, by Francis Chantrey

nave aisle (from 1872, installed 1900) survived the bomb blast. The stained glass in the chantry includes, on the east, a window commemorating Eileen, Countess Stanhope, wife of the seventh earl, designed by the artist Moira Forsyth and dedicated in 1948. The south window, by the same artist (who also designed windows for Guildford Cathedral), presents the arms of seven generations of the Earls Stanhope and of their wives. Scharf's watercolour also records some of the set of emblems carried at the funeral procession of the first earl, from Westminster Abbey to Chevening,

FIG. 102
Memorials in the chantry today

FIG. 103
The Stanhope Chantry, 1880, by George Scharf

S.Scharf del 1880.

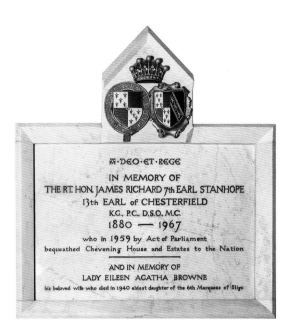

FIG. 104
A slab commemorates the seventh earl,
his countess and his gift to the nation

as installed on the north wall of the chantry on
17 February 1721. The gilt coronet, Earl's Garter
banneret and helm, surcoat, tassels, gauntlets, spurs
and sword were all stolen in 1983; some have been
replaced by replicas.

Above the church font hangs a panel
commemorating the charity established by Lucy,
1st Countess Stanhope, who died on her wedding
anniversary, 24 February 1723, aged thirty. As the
panel explains:

> *The Sum of one Thousand Pounds was Left by the*
> *Right Honourable Lucy Countess Stanhope … the*
> *interest of which is to be applied every Year to the*
> *Putting out Three or more Children of this Parish to*
> *such Trades or Occupations as the Trustees appointed*
> *by the Will of the said Countess Stanhope Shall*
> *Think fit.*

Lucy Stanhope's Charity still offers modest
grants today to help local students with their
education and vocational training.

Facing the churchyard and the rolling hills
beyond is the estate village. One of the cottages
dates from the seventeenth century and its rich
red-orange brickwork give some idea of the
original colour of Chevening, had it not been
necessary to repair its shattered façades in the
1970s. The high brick wall enclosing the estate
dates from soon after 1786.

The close connection between Chevening
and St Botolph's is evident not only in the
graves, monuments, hatchments, furnishings and
general preservation of the church but also from
correspondence in the family's archives. When
Grizel, Countess Stanhope returned after living in
Geneva with her husband and son in 1774 her list
of 'Housekeeper's directions' included:

> As many of the servants as can be spared are
> to go to Church on Sundays, and to take it by
> turns. All to meet at the garden door at the end
> of the arcade, and you and they all go together.

As well as the Stanhope family, some of their
staff were buried in the churchyard. Facing the
east end of the church, for example, is a row
of headstones marking the graves of the estate
steward John Brampton and his family. He
joined Chevening in 1763, died in 1791 and was
succeeded as estate steward by his son, also John,
who died in 1819. Near the door to the Stanhope
Chantry can be found the headstone of the fourth
earl's German valet, Anton Heinrich, and inside
the church there is a wall tablet to the fourth earl's
secretary, George Goodall. Next to the grave of the

seventh earl stand the headstone of his wife and at his feet that of Norah Shotter, his loyal secretary and administrator for forty years, who died in 2001.

Chevening and St Botolph's have many literary associations. Some writers visited when staying with the Stanhopes. For example, the last earl's weekend guests had to join him in attending church on Sunday mornings, an obligation that Rudyard Kipling and his wife did not enjoy. Jane Austen is often assumed to have been inspired by Chevening when writing *Pride and Prejudice* (1813) as she may have stayed with her cousin, the Rev. John Austen, rector of Chevening. The topography of her fictional houses Rosings and Hunsford are similar to the great house and parsonage. One character, Lady Catherine de Burgh, may be based on Grizel, 2nd Countess Stanhope, who lived on at the dower house until she died, aged 92, in 1811, the year Austen wrote her first draft. However, her character may have been based on local legend as her cousin did not become rector until 1813. Jane Austen visited her great uncle, Francis Austen, in Sevenoaks on several occasions before her book was published but there is no record of her staying at Chevening in 1796 (the year she began the novel), as some believe. The house had been concealed from public gaze since the third earl diverted the roads away, in 1786. Whatever the evidence for Chevening as Jane Austen's Rosings Park, one may at least imagine bumping into Mr Darcy on his way to the parsonage.

FIG. 105
The memorial to Philip, 2nd Earl Stanhope
(d. 1786), and his forebears, records their
interment in the family vault

CHAPTER FIVE

The Stanhopes and their Guests

In the pre-Roman Celtic tongue 'Chevening' means 'the people of the ridge': this refers to the crest of Kent's North Downs, but could also serve as a metaphor for a family that held prominent positions in the life of the nation through many generations. The Stanhopes at Chevening originated from Stanhope in County Durham. Eight generations of the family made significant contributions to public life, science and scholarship beyond Chevening. The Hon. Alexander Stanhope was the youngest of the twelve sons of the 1st Earl of Chesterfield and served as a diplomat in the Low Countries and then as British Minister in Madrid (1690–99). His eldest son, the first earl, purchased Chevening while rising to become King George I's Chief Minister. His heir became a noted mathematician. The third earl inherited his love of mathematics and became a pioneer of computers, printing and nautical engineering while also achieving notoriety as a Radical politician in sympathy with the principles of the French Revolution. The fourth earl campaigned against

FIG. 106
Viscount Mahon (later 5th earl) in his Study, 1854, detail of a copy after E.M. Ward painted by A.E. Donkin in 1879, when the sixth earl gave Benjamin Disraeli the original

the new Poor Laws for treating poverty as a crime punishable by confinement in the work house, and championed other causes in the House of Lords. He inherited his father's fascination with new inventions. The fifth earl served as Under Secretary of State for Foreign Affairs and (after declining several diplomatic appointments abroad) became one of Britain's most respected historians. The sixth earl continued the family tradition of contributing to public life through his appointments as Lord Lieutenant of the County of Kent and as First Ecclesiastical Commissioner, responsible for all the Church of England's buildings and investments. The seventh earl served in the Cabinet but he was replaced as First Lord of the Admiralty by Winston Churchill on the outbreak of the Second World War. Politically, the Stanhopes covered the full spectrum, from Radical liberals to ultra-Tories. From the Hon. Alexander Stanhope to the fifth earl, all (except the first earl) were elected Fellows of the Royal Society.

The Stanhope earls also married some remarkable women and had distinguished siblings. They were closely linked with the Pitt family through three marriages – of the first earl to Lucy Pitt (sister of Robert Pitt, MP, father of the Earl of Chatham); of the third earl first to Hester, sister of William Pitt the Younger, and then, as his second wife, to Louisa Grenville, daughter of Lady Chatham's brother. The Earls Stanhope inherited the Chesterfield title in 1952 on the death of the 12th Lord Chesterfield (see below, 'The Stanhopes at Chevening', pp. 138–39).

James, 1st Earl Stanhope (1673–1721)
'The General' (fig. 107) was born in Paris and educated at Eton and Trinity College, Oxford. His army career began in 1691 when, aged eighteen, he served as ADC to the Duke of Schomberg in Italy. During the War of the Spanish Succession he served under Marlborough in Flanders, and in 1704 was sent to Lisbon as a colonel. In 1708 he assumed command of the English forces there. His most notable success was the capture in 1708 of Port Mahon on the island of Minorca, which secured the key naval base for the British fleet in the Mediterranean. His younger brother, Captain Philip Stanhope, was killed leading the marines in the same assault. Two years later Stanhope and his English contingent joined Charles, the Habsburg claimant to the Spanish throne. After victories at Almenara (where Stanhope led a cavalry charge in which he killed the Spanish commander in a "personal encounter" with his own hands) and Zaragosa, the allies reached Madrid in 1710. Three months later they were forced to evacuate the city. Hemmed in at Brihuega with 4,500 men, Stanhope had to surrender. This ended his military career and he spent nearly two years as a prisoner of war in Spain. In February 1711 he wrote from Valladolid: "If I continue long a Prisoner which is not unlikely I shall grow a Philosopher having no other comfort than Books". Fortunately his fears of such a sorry fate soon proved unfounded.

FIG. 107
General James Stanhope, later 1st Earl Stanhope, c.1710, by Michael Dahl

Stanhope had held a Whig seat in Parliament since 1702. Despite his fame as a military hero at the General Election in 1710 he did not secure the seat for Westminster while absent in Spain; humorous attacks by Jonathan Swift (on behalf of the rival Tory candidate) accused Stanhope of blasphemies and homosexuality. Stanhope was reelected MP for Cockermouth in 1711. On returning to England in 1712 he acted vigorously to secure the Hanoverian succession, leading the government's military response to the Jacobite rising in 1715, with the commander-in-chief in Scotland, the Duke of Argyll. King George I made him Secretary of State for the Southern

Department (in 1714) and Leader of the House of Commons. The Southern Secretary of State was responsible for Britain's relations with Spain, France, Italy, the Levant, Ireland and the Colonies. Lord Townshend served as Secretary for the Northern Department, covering Germany, the Low Countries, the Baltic and Russia. Fluent in German, and able to handle the king's other court in Hanover, Stanhope soon held greater influence over the king. As a cosmopolitan polylingual statesman he broke with tradition in preferring personal, face-to-face negotiations with his foreign counterparts, rather than rely on ambassadors and other envoys. This earned Stanhope the sobriquet the 'Knight errant of English diplomacy'.

In November 1716 Stanhope encouraged King George I to increase Britain's influence in Europe as an arbiter between nations. He dismissed the alternative foreign policy as "the old Tory one, that England can subsist by itself, whatever becomes of the rest of Europe, which has been so justly exploited ever since the revolution". Stanhope fell out with Lord Townshend and succeeded him on his dismissal. In 1717 he became the King's Chief Minister (as First Lord of the Treasury and Chancellor of the Exchequer) and his confidant. His 'Quadruple Alliance' in 1718, with the Netherlands, the Holy Roman Empire and France, was soon extended to include Spain. Raised to the peerage as Viscount Stanhope of Mahon (pronounced 'Mahoon') in Minorca in 1717, the following year he was created Earl Stanhope.

He had married in 1713 Lucy Pitt, the daughter of Thomas 'Diamond' Pitt, Governor of Madras, a rich nabob and founder of the Pitt political dynasty. She managed Chevening while Stanhope's duties kept him abroad and in London, and also bore seven children. The first earl made his last visit, "to breathe a little at Chevening", in 1720, spending Christmas in the house. Stanhope lost his temper easily and, during a debate in the House of Lords held on 4 February 1721, while defending the government, he suffered a stroke and collapsed in mid speech. The matter of debate was the South Sea Bubble, the scandal involving the National Debt and inside investments in the South Sea Company made by many senior politicians. He died the next day, at the height of his powers and reputation. On 17 February 1721 in a full military funeral his body was escorted from Westminster to Southwark by two battalions of Foot Guards in a procession including the coaches of King George I, the Prince of Wales and many of the nobility. From Southwark 400 Horse Grenadiers and Life Guards escorted his body to Chevening, where it was interred in the vault beneath the Stanhope Chantry. He is commemorated by a magnificent monument in Westminster Abbey by William Kent and Michael Rysbrack (see figs. 77 and 78), the inscription on which records the *multifarious excellence of his genius*. Unveiled in 1733, the monument was celebrated not only as a work of art to a national hero but also as a way to criticize the new Prime Minister, Robert Walpole, who was guilty of insider trading in the South Sea Company and whose pacifist foreign policy did not advance British mercantile interests abroad.

Philip, 2nd Earl Stanhope (1714–1786)
'The Scientist' (fig. 108) inherited Chevening as a child. Following the advice of his guardian, Philip Dormer Stanhope, 4th Earl of Chesterfield, he was educated in Utrecht, in Geneva, and at a military academy in Turin. With his twin sister he

FIG. 108
Philip, 2nd Eurl Stanhope, 1749, by Allan Ramsay

took up residence at Chevening in 1736. In 1745, as Horace Walpole remarked, Stanhope "lifted up his eyes from Euclid and directed them to matrimony". A happy marriage to Grizel Hamilton, a granddaughter of the 6th Earl of Haddington, produced two sons, Philip and Charles, the latter of whom became the third earl. They lived mainly at Chevening, but also had a house in Hanover Square, until Philip fell ill with consumption. In 1763 the family moved to Geneva for his health, but he died six months later. For the sake of Charles's health and education they remained in Switzerland for ten years, leaving Chevening in the care of a steward, to whom Grizel wrote detailed

instructions. In 1769 their cousin Lord Chatham made Chevening his home for four months. When they returned the second earl sat in the House of Lords as a Whig with marked liberal views. Like Chatham, he opposed war with the American colonies and Chatham wrote of him in 1773: "… were the spirit of liberty lost upon earth it would be found in his heart". The second earl also pursued his interests in science and mathematics. He had edited and published at his own expense Robert Simson's *Principles of Euclid* (1756) and befriended other mathematicians and scientists, including Joseph Priestly and Benjamin Franklin. Considered the best English mathematician of his day, he was elected a Fellow of the Royal Society but modestly declined the presidency.

Charles, 3rd Earl Stanhope (1753–1816)
'Citizen' Stanhope (see fig. 68) inherited his father's enthusiasms for science and democracy. After Eton he studied at the University of Geneva, under Georges-Louis Le Sage for science and mathematics. He was also tutored in art by Jean-Etienne Liotard. Lady Mary Coke, who met him at the age of seventeen, described him as a "genius; his painting would surprise you". He was elected a Fellow of the Royal Society at the age of nineteen. Through his father he met Benjamin Franklin and published in support of his controversial theories (when he was twenty-six) *Principles of Electricity* (1779), which went into French and German editions. His cousin William Pitt the Younger wrote that year that it "will rank him, I supposed, with Dr. Franklin". Stanhope married his cousin Lady Hester Pitt, daughter of Lord Chatham, who wrote of him in 1774: "Lord Mahon is himself a *Mine* richer than all …. I grieve

that he has no seat in Parliament, that wickedest and best school for superior natures". That same year Stanhope contested Westminster as a Radical candidate, inspired by the ideals of John Wilkes, but withdrew during the polling. Lady Hester died in 1780 and the following year he married Louisa Grenville, daughter of Lady Chatham's brother. Finally elected to Parliament in 1780, he made over ninety speeches in his five years there, but fell out with Pitt soon after moving to the Lords in 1786.

Stanhope became increasingly isolated in politics, especially through his sympathies with the principles of the French Revolution. In 1794 his private secretary was arrested, charged with "treasonable practices", and Stanhope's London townhouse in Mansfield Street was torched by a mob. When his secretary was released in December 1794 Stanhope gave "a grand entertainment at … Chevening Hall" (as reported in *The Gentleman's Magazine*) for "near 400 gentlemen and ladies". In the centrepiece of "a large group of emblematic figures was displayed, in large characters, THE RIGHTS OF JURIES". This celebration was intended "to give the people confidence in the justice of our laws, the integrity of our juries, and the independence of our judges". James Gillray caricatured him mercilessly in satirical prints (see fig. 110) and in 1795, following his total failure in the House of Lords to lead and win a debate on opposing the war with France, the 'Stanhope Medal' was struck in tin (fig. 109). It shows on the obverse his head with the inscription *The Minority of One*. Even the king, George III, called Chevening, in jest, "Democracy Hall".

After this, Stanhope returned to his scientific and engineering pursuits. He conducted many experiments at Chevening, using the drawing room

FIG. 109
The Stanhope Medal, 1795,
commemorating 'The Minority of One'

as his laboratory and the canal as his testing tank for his working model boats and mine-sweeper. Many of his inventions were outlets for his political ambitions and were shared for the public good. For example, to reduce the cost of printing and so help the spread of knowledge the third earl designed the first iron printing press, using a lever and screw motion that became standard. In 1777 he invented a calculating machine that influenced the work of Charles Babbage, pioneer of the computer. Two of his machines (dated 1775 and 1777) are in the Science Museum. His stereotype method of printing (using a cast-plate taken from the compositor's individual master letters) he gave to the university presses of Oxford and Cambridge. He also planned canals and championed the development of railways.

At vast personal expense he experimented with steam propulsion for warships. After building a

FIG. 110
'Democratic Leveling – Alliance a la Françoise; – or – The
Union of the Coronet & Clyster-pipe', 1796, by James Gillray

series of steam-powered boats, in 1793 he saw his 200-ton prototype flat-bottomed steamship, H.M.S. Kent, launched at Rotherhithe. This double-bowed cigar shaped 'Ambinavigator', driven by a steam paddle called a 'vibrator', was deemed impractical by the Admiralty. The Navy Board took it out of commission and it was scrapped in 1798. Stanhope also invented and drove a steam carriage, which only ran well when going uphill. Fortunately one of his riskier investigations, into flame-proof buildings, proved successful. Two garden pavilions were erected at Chevening, in one of which guests were served ice creams in the upper floor. To the surprise of onlookers, both temporary structures were then set ablaze; one went up in flames while in the other his guests ate on, oblivious of the fire raging beneath their feet.

Stanhope held many patents. In November 1803 he registered his 'Printing Press and Types' and his "intention to carry on the Business (but not for sale) of a Letter Founder or Maker of Stereotype Plates for Printing, at my Chemical Laboratory in the said Parish". His printing press was installed at Chevening, probably in the Drawing Room, which he called his laboratory. However, despite the drain on the family's fortunes, he did not seek to profit from his inventions. As he ran out of funding, so Stanhope even tried to persuade his eldest son to break the entail that preserved Chevening, but Philip's uncle, William Pitt, told him to refuse.

The greatest cost was to his wife and children. His granddaughter wrote in 1800: "… ardently as he advocated liberty and enfranchisement abroad, he was the sternest of autocrats at home". When his daughter Griselda left home in 1796, aged eighteen, to live in a cottage in Walmer lent by her uncle, William Pitt, Stanhope compared

himself to King Lear. The same year his sixteen-year-old daughter Lucy married the local surgeon in Sevenoaks. The artist James Gillray published a popular print caricaturing the wedding (fig. 110), showing Stanhope giving his daughter away as James Fox reads from Thomas Paine's *Rights of Man* (1791–92) beneath a painting of the execution of the aristocracy in France. In 1800 Stanhope's eldest child, Lady Hester Stanhope, left to live with her maternal grandmother, Lady Chatham. In 1801 and 1802 Hester organized the secret escapes of her three younger stepbrothers, against their father's wishes. Philip was aged nineteen, Charles was sixteen and James had just turned thirteen. Ten years later she wrote, "My father said reading destroyed the faculties of the mind, and carefully locked up his thirty thousand volumes". Stanhope's wife painted copies after Reynolds and Batoni, which the fifth earl later hung with some pride in his study and in his London house. But in 1806 her patience ran out and she left after a legal separation, prompted partly by the advances towards her husband of her Bohemian music teacher, Mrs Walburga Lackner. Stanhope lived with 'Wally' at Chevening, as a recluse, estranged from his heir, until his death in 1816.

Lady Hester Stanhope (fig. 111) acted as hostess for her unmarried uncle, William Pitt the Younger, while he was Prime Minister, both in London and at his official residence, Walmer Castle. There she laid out the gardens. Her nephew, the fifth earl, wrote in his biography of Pitt that while "he came to regard her with almost a father's affection … Mr Pitt was on some occasions much discomposed by her sprightly sallies which did not always spare his own cabinet colleagues". After Pitt died in 1806 she travelled to the Levant and settled in a ruined

FIG. 111
Lady Hester Stanhope, 1810–11, painted in
Constantinople by an unknown artist

monastery at Dar Djoun, near Beirut, for the last twenty-one years of her life. Several biographies have described her as 'The Nun of Lebanon' and 'The Queen of the Desert'. In Lebanon her entourage included dozens of cats and a similar number of wayward native servants. Her memoirs of her adventures, as told to her travelling doctor, were published in six volumes in 1846. She died at her home at Dar Djoun, Lebanon, in 1839 and was buried there. In 1989 her remains were re-interred in the garden of Her Majesty's Ambassador, Beirut at Abey, Mount Lebanon. Subsequently they were disinterred and cremated. Her ashes were finally scattered back at Dar Djoun in 2004 and a

memorial tablet was placed among the tombs of her family in St Botolph's Church, Chevening.

Thanks to Hester her stepbrother James had fled from Chevening and joined the army. The monument by Francis Chantrey in the church at Chevening commemorates James's wife, the daughter of the Earl of Mansfield, who died in childbirth, and features a modest epitaph to her husband, who committed suicide two years later (see chapter 5). Hester's other stepbrother Charles, who fled Chevening with James, joined the army but was killed at the Battle of Corunna in 1809.

Philip, 4th Earl Stanhope (1781–1855)
'The Gardener' (fig. 112) ran away from Chevening in 1801 and enrolled at Erlangen University to evade his father and gain the education he had lacked at home. He wrote in 1805 that he had been "delivered from the House of Bondage" to the "promised land". He remained in Germany, his favourite country, as a young man. In a lawsuit launched in 1806 he accused his father of reducing the value of Chevening by £80,000 by selling farms and timber. It continued until 1812 and he only returned to Chevening after the death of his father in 1816. At Chevening his passions turned to the development and planting of the gardens. A German guest wrote that Stanhope "has endeavored to introduce German habits, German domestic arrangements, and a German tone of society into his house … even the hour of dining was an approach to ours". The new earl inherited his father's eccentricities. His maiden speech in the House of Lords so offended the French that it provoked pamphlets in Paris, where his brother James found he needed an armed escort. As Viscount Mahon he had married Catherine Smith,

FIG. 112
Philip, 4th Earl Stanhope, c.1803, by William Owen

and agriculture. His involvement with extremist movements led to the interception and destruction of his correspondence, as recorded in Home Office files. As vice-president of the Society of Arts, under Prince Albert, he was offered a commemorative medal in 1852 following the success of the Great Exhibition in the Crystal Palace, but he refused to accept it, writing "I very much disapproved of the event". Like his father, he had a wide range of interests, from teetotalism to aviation. While objecting to the spread of railways he invested (unwisely) in the creation of a flying machine and in an 'Aerial Courier Company'. A great traveller, he wrote guidebooks to Switzerland and Italy and contributed to Murray's handbooks to Germany. His grandson, Lord Rosebery, succeeded Gladstone as Prime Minister.

Philip Henry, 5th Earl Stanhope (1805–1875) 'The Historian' (fig. 106) was tutored at home before going up to Oxford with his younger brother in 1822. He was elected a Fellow of the Royal Society in 1827. He served as Under Secretary of State for Foreign Affairs under the Duke of Wellington in Peel's government in 1834, and was offered the same position in 1841 but declined it. Two years later he declined the role of ambassador to Spain. Stanhope held out for a government position. In 1845 Peel offered him the Secretaryship of the Board of Control for India, which he also declined but later held briefly before Peel's government fell. In 1858 he was offered the embassy at either St Petersburg or Vienna, but declined both, saying he was too old (at fifty-three). The highest position he was offered was that of Chancellor of the Duchy of Lancaster, which came with the approval of Queen Victoria,

daughter of the 1st Lord Carrington, in 1803, but he continued visiting Germany alone (with his German valet) for many years. His involvement in German affairs led him in 1831 to adopt the cause and gain custody of Kaspar Hauser, a supposed foundling from Nuremberg who became the boy pretender to the Grand Duchy of Baden. When Kaspar died in 1833 from a self-inflicted wound, Stanhope was blamed and had to publish *Tracts relating to Caspar Hauser* (1836) to clear his name and distance himself from the boy's claims.

The fourth earl campaigned vociferously against the Poor Law and Free Trade and was a staunch supporter of the protection of British industry but he declined that as well. Like his father and grandfather, he contributed to the political life of the nation mainly through the House of Lords, where he preserved his political independence. His second son, Edward, became a prominent politician who held many offices, including Under Secretary of State for India, Secretary of State for the Colonies, Secretary of State for War and President of the Board of Trade.

Stanhope felt his career as a statesman had been unfulfilled but he became a great historian. Writing as Viscount Mahon, he is best known for his *Notes of Conversations with the Duke of Wellington* (1888). His major works of scholarship are *The War of the Succession in Spain, 1702–1714* (1832), his seven-volume *History of England* (1836–54) covering the years 1713 to 1783, and his life of his cousin, William Pitt the Younger (1861). In these he drew heavily on documents preserved at Chevening. His additions to these papers include a volume of letters written by the 4th Earl of Chesterfield that he obtained from his publisher as an honorarium for editing Chesterfield's letters (five volumes, 1845–53). Charles Darwin lived nearby at Down House, just outside the village of Downe, and a presentation copy of his *Origin of Species* (1859) is also in the Chevening library.

Stanhope was a keen collector of family portraits (see Chapter 3). From 1844 he served on Prince Albert's Commission on the Fine Arts, responsible for the interior decoration of the Palace of Westminster. In 1846 he was elected President of the Society of Antiquaries, a position he held for nearly thirty years; it carried with it membership of the governing bodies of the British Museum and the Royal Academy. The founder and chairman of the National Portrait Gallery, he was also President of the Royal Literary Fund and a founding member of the Historical Manuscripts Commission; he was personally responsible for the Copyrights Act. An outstanding historian, while an Examiner in the School of Law and Modern History at Oxford University he founded the Stanhope Essay Prize. Following his marriage in 1834 he took a long lease on a town house in Grosvenor Place, which the family kept until after the death of the sixth countess in 1923.

Arthur, 6th Earl (1838–1905)

'The Lord Lieutenant' (fig. 113) was educated at Harrow and served in the Grenadier Guards. He became a friend of the Prince of Wales (later King Edward VII) in Switzerland in 1857, when Stanhope was aged nineteen and the prince sixteen. Family tradition held that his career prospects in the army were ended by Prince Albert following the Prince of Wales's brief affair with a Dublin actress. Nellie Clifden had been smuggled into Stanhope's quarters (in his absence) while the young prince was staying with the Guards near Dublin in August 1861. In 1868 Stanhope was elected MP for Leominster. The following year he married Evelyn Pennefather, daughter of the Secretary to the Viceroy in Ireland; their wedding was a great social occasion, with Disraeli proposing the toast to the bride and groom. In 1874 he was appointed a Junior Lord of the Treasury, and became a Government Whip under Disraeli; in 1878 he accepted the position of First Ecclesiastical Commissioner, which he held for twenty-five years, managing the Church of England's properties and investments. In 1890 he was appointed Lord Lieutenant of the county of Kent. Lady Stanhope was an influential political hostess.

FIG. 113
Arthur, 6th Earl Stanhope, 1915, posthumous painting by Leon Sprink

The sixth earl's youngest brother, Philip James Stanhope (1847–1923), continued the family tradition of diplomatic service through an international career as a politician, for which he was raised to the peerage as 1st Lord Weardale. He is buried in the Stanhope plot at St Botolph's, where his headstone reads: *A life-long friend of International Peace. For ten years, from 1912 to 1922, President of the Inter-Parliamentary Union for the prevention of war and one of the founders of the Union.* As well as leading this global forum for dialogue between nations he was also, with Lord Curzon, president of the National League for Opposing Woman Suffrage. His nephew, the seventh earl, inherited Weardale Manor, the 145-room house he built in Kent.

James Richard, 7th Earl Stanhope and 13th Earl of Chesterfield (1880–1967)

'The Last Earl' (fig. 114) was educated at Eton and Magdalen College, Oxford. In 1901 he was commissioned into the Grenadier Guards and was posted to South Africa. On his father's death in April 1905 he inherited the remaining family estates, keeping those in Kent (3,500 acres) but selling off those in Devon (5,000 acres) and Derbyshire (2,400 acres). On the outbreak of the First World War he rejoined his regiment and served in France until he was transferred to the General Staff. Promoted to Lieutenant Colonel, he was awarded the Military Cross and the Distinguished Service Order. His only brother, Richard, was killed during the Battle of the Somme.

In 1921 Stanhope married Eileen Browne (fig. 115), daughter of the 5th Marquis of Sligo. During the 1920s and 1930s they made Chevening a centre for political and social activity, with Winston Churchill among their many distinguished guests. In 1923 Stanhope was appointed Civil Lord of the Admiralty, a post in which he clashed with Churchill, then Chancellor of the Exchequer, over Churchill's pruning of expenditure on the Fleet (a criticism that Churchill later denied). Nevertheless the two men remained friends and neighbours, as Churchill's house, Chartwell, is only four miles from Chevening.

The 1920s provides one of the many historic precedents for Chevening's more recent role, as a seat of diplomacy, for in that decade the house was at the heart of Britain's debate over the nation's future place in the world. Rudyard Kipling was a frequent guest (his home, Bateman's, is a short drive away). His biographer, Andrew Lycett, has

FIG. 114
James, 7th Earl Stanhope, c.1937, by James Gunn

written about a 'Chevening set', and how, as "one of the youngest pre-war 'die-hard' Conservatives, Stanhope played host to an eclectic group of latter-day imperialists at Chevening … weekend parties were usually well seeded with reactionary generals and admirals". Kipling was there in December 1921, when the Chief of the Imperial General Staff, Sir Henry Wilson, was informed at Chevening of the signing of the Anglo-Irish treaty; General Sir Claud Jacob, Chief of the General Staff in India, saw the domino effect on the Empire, and replied: "Well, that means we shall lose India". Five years later Kipling had a meeting with the Australian Prime Minister, S.M. Bruce, at Chevening during the Imperial Conference that devised the Commonwealth as a free trade relationship between Britain and the former colonies.

When in 1930 Stanhope was offered, informally, the position of Governor General of Canada, he declined, preferring to continue his career at Westminster. After the fall of Ramsay MacDonald's Labour Government in 1931, Stanhope served again at the Admiralty, at the War Office and at the Foreign Office. In 1934 King George V conferred on Stanhope the Order of the Garter. That same year he helped to establish the National Maritime Museum (its name came from Kipling, as an alternative to the 'National Nautical and Naval Museum'). In 1936 Stanhope achieved his ambition of a Cabinet post: as First Commissioner of Works he had to organize the Coronation ceremonies of 1937. He now found himself at the heart of the Abdication Crisis, when the Coronation of Edward VIII had to be cancelled in favour of that of his brother, the Duke of York. Stanhope had been invited to Buckingham Palace to meet the Prince of Wales's intended wife, Mrs Simpson, but maintained the government's position. When he entertained the Duke of York at Chevening the future queen thanked Stanhope for helping her husband to relax. At the Coronation of George VI Stanhope had the honour of being one of the four Garter Knights to carry the canopy of Coronation.

From the Office of Works Stanhope transferred to the Presidency of the Board of Education. In the wake of the Munich crisis of September 1938 he returned to the Admiralty as First Lord, where he selected personally the senior officers who were to hold the key naval commands during the Second Word War. On the outbreak of war Churchill returned to the Admiralty and Stanhope was appointed Lord President of the Council. Churchill wrote to Stanhope, asking "to learn from you the points you had specially in mind in order that nothing may be overlooked in changing guard … I hope that we are to be colleagues as well as neighbours". Stanhope also served as Leader of the House of Lords (1938-40) and as President of the Council (1939-40). Knowing that his wife was dying from cancer Stanhope withdrew from public life in 1940, aged sixty.

He continued to attend the House of Lords and served as chairman of the Standing Committee on Museums and Galleries (1941-48). He served as a trustee of the National Portrait Gallery (1930-60), like his grandfather before him, and as a trustee of the Chantrey Bequest (from 1927 until 1963), which purchases British art for the nation. He also chaired the National Maritime Museum (1934-59). At Chevening he supervised the estate and sorted the family papers while his loyal secretary for nearly forty years, Miss Norah Shotter, kept any aspirant seventh countesses at bay.

Chevening was fortunate to survive the Second World War for it stands close to the RAF airfield at Biggin Hill. Another prime target closer by must have been Fort Halstead, home since 1938 to the military's rockets research programme (and later the birthplace of Britain's atomic bomb). In 1941 a German bomb fell into Chevening but failed to explode (it can be seen, defused, in the Kitchen). St Botolph's had its windows blown out. Chevening's dower house, Ovenden, was hit and destroyed. In 1943 Stanhope visited 10 Downing Street and discussed with Churchill his idea of offering Chevening to the nation. Having no heir and foreseeing that future politicians might not be

FIG. 115
Eileen, 7th Countess Stanhope, 1921, by Philip de Laszlo

so well placed as he had been, Stanhope arranged for the house and estate to pass on his death to a trust, to be preserved for the nation in perpetuity and continue at the heart of British political life. In 1959, Parliament passed the Chevening Estate Act. The seventh Earl Stanhope died in 1967 in his eighty-seventh year, closing 250 years of the Stanhope family at Chevening.

The Chevening Trust

The Chevening Estate Act of 1959 (amended 1987) established and empowered a board of trustees to preserve Chevening – the house, its contents and the estate – independent of the public purse, and to manage it as a country residence for a person nominated by the Prime Minister. Chevening also serves as a memorial to the Stanhope family, who lived here from 1717 to 1967. The Act came into force on the death of the seventh earl in 1967, when the trustees took over responsibility for the house and the estate, with all the powers in that behalf of an absolute owner. The Board of Trustees is chaired by the Lord Privy Seal and includes the Director of the Victoria and Albert Museum, two persons appointed by the Prime Minister (one of whom must be experienced in estate management and forestry), one by the Secretary of State for Environment, Food and Rural Affairs, and other trustees. The Board is not an agent or servant of the Crown. All the costs of the house are met from the Trust's own resources arising from Lord Stanhope's bequest.

Under the terms of the Act the Prime Minister has the responsibility of nominating an individual to occupy the house (with his or her immediate family). This person can be the Prime Minister, a minister who is a member of the Cabinet, a lineal descendant of King George VI, or the spouse, widow or widower of such a descendant. Should the Prime Minister be unable to identify a suitable 'Nominated Person' the house may be used by the Canadian High Commissioner or the American Ambassador. If none wish to take up the option, ultimately Chevening would pass into the care of the National Trust. Since 1980 Chevening has become by convention the country home of the Foreign Secretary. To date the persons so nominated have been (as known at the time of their nomination):

Anthony Barber	1973
The Lord Hailsham	1973–74
HRH The Prince of Wales	1974–80
The Lord Carrington	1981–82
Francis Pym	1982–83
Sir Geoffrey Howe	1983–89
John Major	1989
Douglas Hurd	1989–95
Malcolm Rifkind	1995–97
Robin Cook	1997–2001
Jack Straw	2001–06
Margaret Beckett	2006–07
David Miliband	2007–10
William Hague (alternating nomination)	2010–14
Nick Clegg (alternating nomination)	2010–14
Philip Hammond	2014–16
Boris Johnson	2016 to present

The Chevening Scholars and Fellows

Chevening is the appropriate title chosen in 1984 for the British Government's international awards scheme aimed at developing global leaders. Funded by the Foreign and Commonwealth Office (FCO) and partner organisations, Chevening offers two types of award – Chevening Scholarships and Chevening Fellowships – the recipients of which are personally selected by British Embassies and High Commissions. Chevening offers a unique opportunity for future leaders, influencers and decision-makers from all over the world to develop professionally and academically, network extensively, experience British culture and build lasting positive relationships with the United Kingdom. While the Chevening Secretariat forms part of the Association of Commonwealth Universities in Woburn House in London, events are sometimes organized at Chevening, such as the scheme's 30th anniversary celebration in 2014 at which 800 alumni and current scholars from across the world were entertained in the house and garden.

Further Reading

Most of the Stanhope family papers are on long loan to the Kent History and Library Centre (formerly known as Kent Archives Office) in Maidstone. Much remains in the Library at Chevening. Copies of Bradshaw's account to Earl Stanhope, 2 February 1736/37, of the inventories of 1723 and 1753 and of payments to Lord Londonderry in 1726 are held in the Department of Furniture, Textiles and Fashion at the Victoria and Albert Museum. The inventories of 1876, 1905 and 1926 remain in the house Library. Most of the quotations by and about the family in this book are taken from the family papers and from Aubrey Newman, *The Stanhopes of Chevening* (London, 1969) where the sources are cited.

Badeslade, T., *Thirty six different views of noblemen and gentlemen's seats in the county of Kent*, London, 1750

Banks, E., 'Restoring an ageing landscape. Changes in the Gardens at Chevening', *Country Life*, vol. 166, no. 4289 (20 September 1979), pp. 850–52

Bold, J., *John Webb*, Oxford, 1989, pp.154–55

Brackett, O., 'Furniture at Chevening House – II', *Old Furniture*, vol. 7 (May-August 1929), pp. 69–76

Bryant, J., 'Exempla Vertutis: Designs for Sculpture', in S. Soros, ed., *William Kent*, New Haven and London, 2013, pp. 559–62

Campbell, C ., *Vitruvius Britannicus*, vol. 2, London, 1717

Chevening, *List of Portraits and Busts in the Principal Rooms at Chevening*, London, 1856, and rev. edns 1867, 1871, 1931

Chevening Parish History Group, *The History of the Parish of Chevening*, Sevenoaks, 1999

Cleveland, C. W. Vane, Duchess of, *The Life & Letters of Lady Hester Stanhope. By her Niece the Duchess of Cleveland*, London 1914

Colvin, H., and Newman, J., *Of Building. Roger North's Writings on Architecture*, Oxford, 1981

Downer, M., *The Earl's Machine. The portable calculator invented by Charles, 3rd Earl Stanhope*, London, 2008

Gomme, A., 'Chevening: the Big Issues', *The Georgian Group Journal*, vol. 14, (2004), pp. 167–86

Gomme, A., 'Chevening: the Resolutions', *The Georgian Group Journal*, vol. 15 (2006), pp. 121–39

Goodall, J., 'Seat of British diplomacy. Chevening House, Kent', *Country Life*, vol. 206, no. 9 (29 February 2012), pp. 52–56

Goodall, J., 'Stairway to Heaven', *Country Life*, vol. 209, no. 29 (15 July 2015), pp. 56–59

Gooch, G. P., and Stanhope, G., *The Life of Charles, Third Earl Stanhope*, London,1914

Gotch, J. A., 'Some Newly Found Drawings and Letters of John Webb', *Journal of the RIBA*, vol. 28 (1921), pp. 565–81 (letter V)

Harris, J., *The History of Kent*, London, 1719, vol. I, p. 74

Howes, J., *On Citizen Stanhope and his Iron Hand Press*, Westerham, 2003

Hurd, J., 'Cricket with the Dutch Foreign Minister', *Country Life*, vol. 200, no. 37 (14 September 2006), pp. 138–41

Hussey, C., 'A Great Gift to the Nation. Chevening, Kent', *Country Life*, vol. 143, no. 3698 (18 January 1968), pp. 102–04

Mayer, J., *Philip Henry, Lord Stanhope: der Gegenspieler Kaspar Hausers*, Stuttgart 1988

Mills, M. (ed.), *Your Most Dutyfull Servant: the correspondence between Grizel, Countess Stanhope of Chevening in Kent and John Brampton, her steward, between the years 1764 and 1774*, Sevenoaks, 1992

N. A. D. F. A. S., *Record of Church Furnishings: St. Botolph's Church, Chevening, Kent*, London, 1986

Newman, A., *The Stanhopes of Chevening*, London, 1969

Newman, J., *The Buildings of England. Kent: West and the Weald*, New Haven and London, 2012, pp.164–69

Oswald, A., 'The Story of Chevening. Lord Stanhope's Gift to the Nation', *Country Life*, vol. 125, no. 3256 (11 June 1959), pp. 1312–15

Penny, N. B., 'English Church Monuments to Women who died in Childbed between 1780 and 1835', *Journal of the Warburg and Courtauld Institutes*, vol. 38 (1975), pp. 314–32

Pitt, W., *Lord Chatham at Chevening: 1769*, London, 1855

Robinson, S., 'Chevening House', *Archaeologica Cantiana*, vol. 16 (1886), pp. 127–33

Robinson, S., *Chevening Church and Chevening House*, London, 1891

Shuff, D., 'A House Fit for a Prince?', *Woman's Journal* (19 November 1976), pp. 69–71

Simon, J., 'Allan Ramsay and picture frames', *Burlington Magazine*, vol. 136 (July, 1994), pp. 444–55

Smart, A., *Allan Ramsay, painter, essayist and man of the Enlightenment*, New Haven and London, 1992

Smithers, D. W., *Jane Austen in Kent*, Westerham 1981

Sotheby's, *Chevening, Sevenoaks, Kent*, 10 May 1993

Stanhope, G., *The Life of Charles, 3rd Earl Stanhope*, London, 1914

Stanhope, H., *Memoirs of the Lady Hester Stanhope, as related by herself in Conversations with her Physician*, 3 vols., London, 1846

Stanhope, H., *Travels of Lady Hester Stanhope, forming the Completion of her Memoirs. Narrated by her Physician*, London, 1846

Stewart, J. D., 'John and John Baptist Closterman: some documents', *Burlington Magazine*, vol. 106 (1964), pp. 306–09

Strange, E. F., 'Furniture at Chevening House – I', *Old Furniture*, vol. 6, no. 22 (March 1929), pp. 125–32

Tipping, H. A., 'The Chevening Library', *Country Life*, vol. 47, no. 1218 (8 May 1920), pp. 627–29

Tipping, H. A., *English Homes: Early Georgian, 1714–1760*, vol. 1, London 1921

Tolley, S., 'In Praise of General Stanhope: Reputation, Public Opinion and the Battle of Almenar, 1710–1733', *British Journal for Military History*, vol. 3, no. 2 (February 2017), pp. 1–13

Williams, B., *Stanhope: A Study in Eighteenth-Century War and Diplomacy*, Oxford, 1932

Wilson, M. I., *A House of Distinction. The Stanhopes and Chevening*, Sevenoaks, 2011

Wood, L., 'William Hallett's lantern stand for Chevening', *Furniture History*, vol. 41 (2005), pp. 21–24

Wyld, H., 'A princely gift', *Country Life*, vol. 206, no. 9 (29 February 2012), pp. 57–59

Young, W., *Town and Country Mansions and Suburban Houses*, London, 1879

The Stanhopes of Chevening
and their links with the Pitts

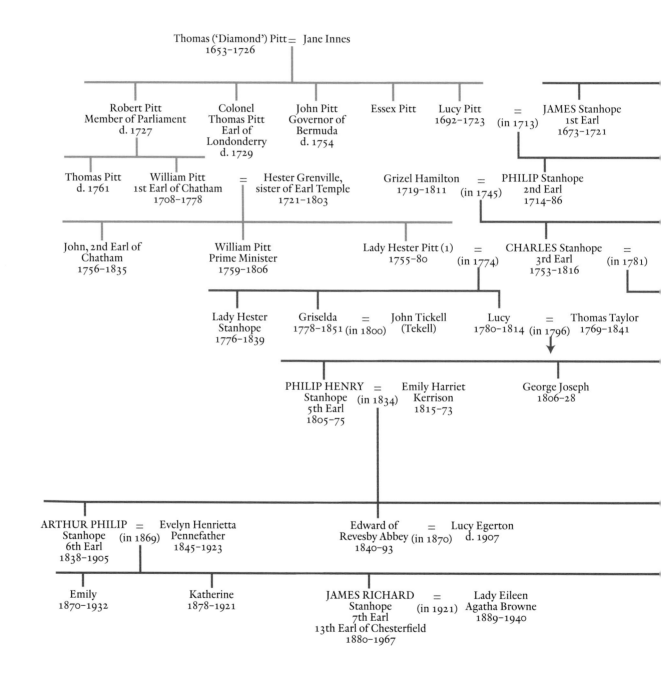

Thomas ('Diamond') Pitt = Jane Innes
1653–1726

Robert Pitt
Member of Parliament
d. 1727

Colonel
Thomas Pitt
Earl of
Londonderry
d. 1729

John Pitt
Governor of
Bermuda
d. 1754

Essex Pitt

Lucy Pitt
1692–1723

= (in 1713)

JAMES Stanhope
1st Earl
1673–1721

Thomas Pitt
d. 1761

William Pitt
1st Earl of Chatham
1708–1778

= Hester Grenville,
sister of Earl Temple
1721–1803

Grizel Hamilton
1719–1811

= (in 1745)

PHILIP Stanhope
2nd Earl
1714–86

John, 2nd Earl of
Chatham
1756–1835

William Pitt
Prime Minister
1759–1806

Lady Hester Pitt (1)
1755–80

= (in 1774)

CHARLES Stanhope
3rd Earl
1753–1816

= (in 1781)

Lady Hester
Stanhope
1776–1839

Griselda
1778–1851 (in 1800)

= John Tickell
(Tekell)

Lucy
1780–1814 (in 1796)

= Thomas Taylor
1769–1841

PHILIP HENRY
Stanhope
5th Earl
1805–75

= (in 1834)

Emily Harriet
Kerrison
1815–73

George Joseph
1806–28

ARTHUR PHILIP
Stanhope
6th Earl
1838–1905

= (in 1869)

Evelyn Henrietta
Pennefather
1845–1923

Edward of
Revesby Abbey
1840–93

= (in 1870)

Lucy Egerton
d. 1907

Emily
1870–1932

Katherine
1878–1921

JAMES RICHARD
Stanhope
7th Earl
13th Earl of Chesterfield
1880–1967

= (in 1921)

Lady Eileen
Agatha Browne
1889–1940

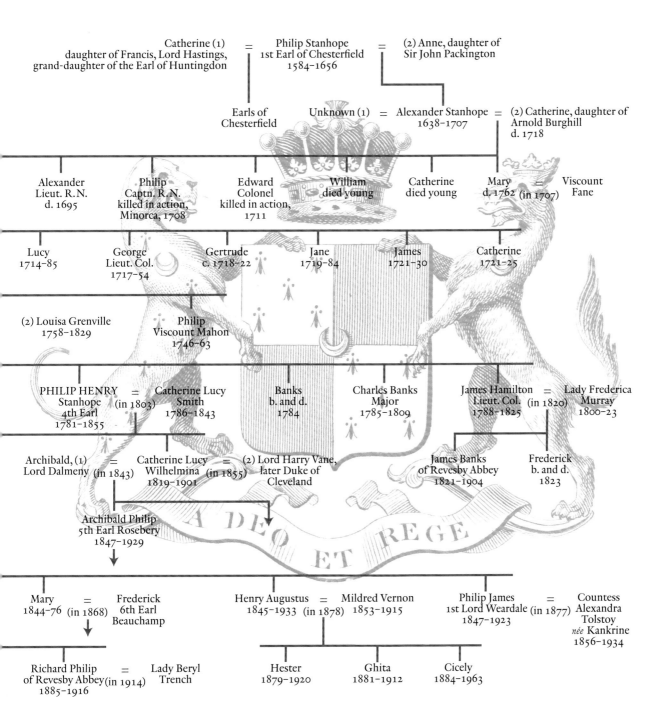

Catherine (1)
daughter of Francis, Lord Hastings,
grand-daughter of the Earl of Huntingdon
= Philip Stanhope
1st Earl of Chesterfield
1584–1656
= (2) Anne, daughter of
Sir John Packington

Earls of
Chesterfield

Unknown (1) = Alexander Stanhope
1638–1707
= (2) Catherine, daughter of
Arnold Burghill
d. 1718

Alexander
Lieut. R.N.
d. 1695

Philip
Captn. R.N.
killed in action,
Minorca, 1708

Edward
Colonel
killed in action,
1711

William
died young

Catherine
died young

Mary
d. 1762 (in 1707)
= Viscount
Fane

Lucy
1714–85

George
Lieut. Col.
1717–54

Gertrude
c. 1718–22

Jane
1719–84

James
1721–30

Catherine
1721–25

(2) Louisa Grenville
1758–1829

Philip
Viscount Mahon
1746–63

PHILIP HENRY
Stanhope
4th Earl
1781–1855
= (in 1803)
Catherine Lucy
Smith
1786–1843

Banks
b. and d.
1784

Charles Banks
Major
1785–1809

James Hamilton
Lieut. Col.
1788–1825
= (in 1820)
Lady Frederica
Murray
1800–23

Archibald, (1)
Lord Dalmeny
= (in 1843)
Catherine Lucy
Wilhelmina
1819–1901
= (in 1855) (2) Lord Harry Vane,
later Duke of
Cleveland

James Banks
of Revesby Abbey
1821–1904

Frederick
b. and d.
1823

Archibald Philip
5th Earl Rosebery
1847–1929

Mary
1844–76 (in 1868)
= Frederick
6th Earl
Beauchamp

Henry Augustus
1845–1933 (in 1878)
= Mildred Vernon
1853–1915

Philip James
1st Lord Weardale
1847–1923
= (in 1877) Countess
Alexandra
Tolstoy
née Kankrine
1856–1934

Richard Philip
of Revesby Abbey (in 1914)
1885–1916
= Lady Beryl
Trench

Hester
1879–1920

Ghita
1881–1912

Cicely
1884–1963

A Concise Chronology

1551	John Lennard purchases the Chevening estate for £420
1613	Estate map drawn by George Batcheler, includes the Tudor house
c.1629	New house completed for Richard Lennard, 13th Lord Dacre, probably designed by Inigo Jones
c.1655	John Webb designs "Lord Dacre's Noble Room"
1679	Estate map drawn by Richard Browne, with views of the house and garden
c.1680	Entrance hall moved from south to north side
1688–1700	The Earl of Sussex enlarges the garden into the park through extensive planting of trees, and probably forms the canal
1717	The house is illustrated by Colen Campbell in Vitruvius Britannicus, volume two
1717, June	The Chevening estate sold by the Earl of Sussex's daughters to General James Stanhope for £28,000
c.1718–25	Thomas Fort extends the house with pedimented wings and flanking pavilions. Zachariah Gisbourn encloses the forecourt with wrought iron railings. Formal gardens extended to south and structured with allees
1719	House and gardens illustrated in John Harris, History of Kent
1721–23	Nicholas Dubois installs new staircase
1736	The second earl takes up residence and creates the Tapestry Room with tapestries presented to the first earl and new furniture supplied by William Bradshaw
1765–75	Second earl and family live in Geneva
1769	'Chatham's Ride', a scenic drive through the escarpment wood in the North Park, planned while William Pitt, 1st Earl of Chatham in residence
1775–78	Gardens remodelled as picturesque landscape
1776–77	The hipped roof is replaced by a blocked attic storey
1786	Third earl inherits. He has the house exterior encased with mathematical tiles and adds pilasters to main fronts (1786–88)
1816	Fourth earl inherits the house "standing in a hayfield", undertakes extensive repairs to the roof and attic storey (1817) and creates formal garden features
1855	Fifth earl inherits, removes sash bars from windows (c.1860); expands and rearranges the collection of family portraits; builds new stable block (1860)
1875	Sixth earl inherits. William Young remodels the Drawing Room c.1878, and adds the Billiard Room
1905	Seventh earl inherits. He modernizes the domestic offices (1912), constructs the Loggia (c.1920), brings the Chatham Vase from Revesby Abbey and extends the ha-ha as its setting (1934)
1959	The Chevening Estate Act is passed by Parliament
1967	Death of seventh earl
1969–75	The Trustees undertake complete renovation with Donald Insall and Associates, replacing the attic with a hipped roof and dormers, removing mathematical tiles, refacing with new brickwork, and adding a pediment to the north front. John Fowler advises on interior redecoration
1979 –present	The Trustees commission Elizabeth Banks to initiate a gradual restoration of the gardens and park, emphasizing important features from successive preceding periods of design (such as the north avenue, replanted after the storm of 1987) within a harmonious whole, which continues to this day. Edward Bulmer advises on interior redecoration

A Walk in the Park

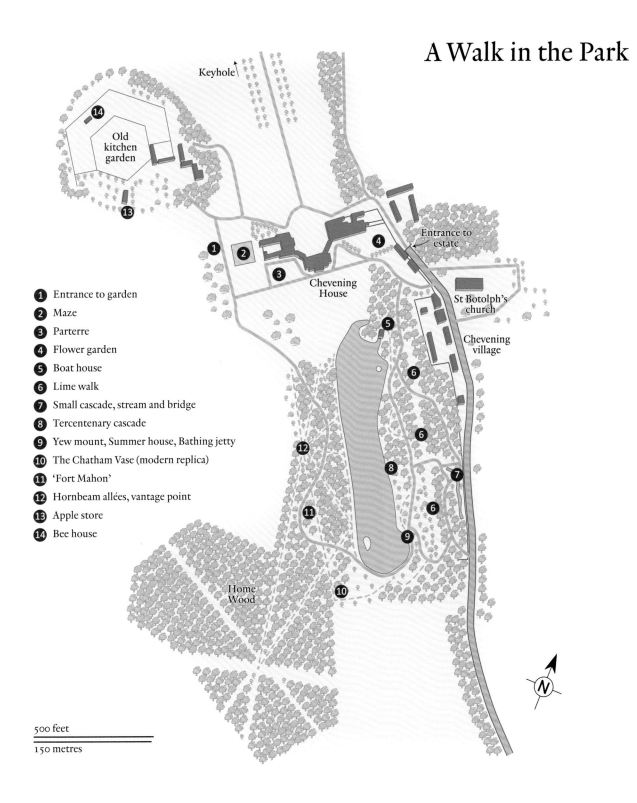

Keyhole

Old kitchen garden

14

13

Entrance to estate

Chevening House

St Botolph's church

Chevening village

1 Entrance to garden
2 Maze
3 Parterre
4 Flower garden
5 Boat house
6 Lime walk
7 Small cascade, stream and bridge
8 Tercentenary cascade
9 Yew mount, Summer house, Bathing jetty
10 The Chatham Vase (modern replica)
11 'Fort Mahon'
12 Hornbeam allées, vantage point
13 Apple store
14 Bee house

Home Wood

500 feet

150 metres

N

Acknowledgements

It is a truth universally acknowledged that a house in possession of a good collection must be in want of a monograph. The quality of Chevening's collection of paintings, furniture and decorative arts and the Library, warrants a full catalogue. This slim volume is intended only as an introductory overview, produced as a contribution to the celebrations in July 2017 marking the tercentenary of the creation of the Stanhope title and the fiftieth anniversary of the Chevening Trust. The family's own distinguished historian, the fifth earl, published concise room-by-room visitor guides to the paintings and busts as he rearranged the collection from 1856. In the twentieth century the family's fascinating history was the subject of a book by Aubrey Newman, commissioned by the last earl. Since then, surprisingly little research has been undertaken into the collection itself, for one of such importance. When the house passed from the Stanhope family to the trustees fifty years ago, in 1967, the priority for research was the building itself, the interior decoration and gardens, prior to restoration. In the 1970s Donald Insall pioneered the full understanding of the building and Elizabeth Banks drew up a masterplan for the gardens. Later, John Martin Robinson and Edward Bulmer made researched recommendations for the presentation of the interiors. More recently, research led by Andor Gomme has focussed on the question of Inigo Jones's contribution as architect; Lucy Wood has published on William Hallett's furniture and Helen Wyld on the tapestries. Michael Wilson's book on the Stanhopes and Chevening was published in 2011.

My first thanks are to Edward Barham, Chairman of the Trustees' Finance and General Purposes Committee and to Colonel Alastair Mathewson, O.B.E., Secretary to the Board of Trustees, who together commissioned this book. Their proposal was enthusiastically welcomed by the trustees. To Donald Insall I am most grateful for sharing his recollections, providing access to his company's project archive and for reading the draft manuscript. The Baroness Rawlings, Edward Barham and Lord Sackville read and advised on the text on behalf of the trustees. Alastair Mathewson made many additions based on his own expertise and research. The other readers to whom I am indebted for encouragement (and corrections) are Chevening's past and present librarians, Michael Wilson and James Bettley. Any errors that eluded the readers' scrutiny are entirely my responsibility.

At the V&A I am most grateful to three successive directors, Mark Jones, Martin Roth and Tristram Hunt, for nominating me to serve as their representative on the Board of Trustees. Among the V&A curators and librarians who have kindly visited to share their expertise on site I am especially grateful to Angus Patterson and Elizabeth James. Alvaro Soler del Campo from the Royal Armoury in Madrid identified the monogram on the armour on the staircase. Once again I am indebted to Nazek Ghaddar for making sense of my manuscript and for securing many illustrations. Most of the research and writing was done away from the V&A and I am grateful to Barbara and Max Bryant for letting the Stanhopes into our home. Max was especially helpful in researching the collection of Roman tombstones.

At Chevening Colonel Mathewson's team could not have been more helpful and hospitable over the years, and I would like to thank Colonel Richard Brook, Kay Thorne, Judith Edwards, Lesley Creasey, Jane Taylor, Bernadette and Michael Walker, Rob Emmett, Paul and Hilda Willard, Chris and Leisa Coombs, Harvey and Mandy Smoker, Wayne and Sharon Parsonage, Andy and Janet Curtis, Mark Wilkinson and William Lucy.

Hattie Young and Richard Valencia took many of the new photographs for this publication. Laura Parker's design skills are evident throughout. Paul Holberton was the trustees' first choice as publisher and has produced a beautiful book to his usual outstanding standards and in time for the tercentenary celebrations. JB

Index

Numbers are page numbers, in italics indicating works by, in grey indicating portraits